The *Off-* Bicycle Book

Iain Lynn

Contributing Editor
Stan Abbott

Technical Editor
David Wrath-Sharman

Second edition revised and updated by Tom Bogdanowicz

Cover picture by Stan Abbott, taken near Gunnerside,
Swaledale, courtesy of the Keld Mountain Bike Centre

AUTHOR'S DEDICATION: To KP, for patience above and beyond the call of duty, to the BT Crew for putting up with me, to PRL
for at least trying to put up with me, and to TL and EL for putting up
with even more.

First edition published 1987 by Leading Edge Press and Publishing,
The Old Chapel, Burtersett, Hawes, North Yorkshire, DL8 3PB.
Tel (096 97) 566. ISBN 0-948135-02-6

Second, revised and updated edition, July 1989
Second Impression, January 1990
© 1987, 1989 Iain Lynn and Leading Edge Press and Publishing

British Library Cataloguing in Publication Data

Lynn, Iain
    The Off-Road Bicycle Book
    1. All terrain cycling
    I. Title II. Wrath-Sharman, David
    III. Crane, Richard, *1953-* IV. Abbott, Stan
    796.6'0914'3

    ISBN 0-948135-09-3

Design: Stan Abbott (Journalism)
Cartoons: Bill Lehan
Cartography: Geoff Apps and Ruth Abbott
Type: Leading Edge Press & Publishing
Printed and bound in Great Britain by H Shanley (Printers) Ltd,
Bolton

The publisher wishes to thank Gabriel Nichols for additional help
and advice.

The detailed maps in this book are based upon Ordnance Survey
maps with the permission of the Controller of HMSO, Crown
copyright reserved.

Contents

Chapters by Iain Lynn, unless otherwise stated

Bibliography and recommended reading

Books

Van der Plas, R. **The Mountain Bike Book,** 1984. Velo Press Inc, New York

Bicycling Magazine's **All-Terrain Bikes,** Rodale Press Inc, Emmanaus, Pennsylvania

Crane, Richard and Nicholas. **Bicycles up Kilimanjaro,** 1985. Oxford Illustrated Press, Somerset

Haldane, A.R.B. **The Drove Roads of Scotland,** 1952. David and Charles, Newton Abbott

Godwin, F. and Toulson, S. **The Drovers' Roads of Wales,** 1977. Wildwood House, London

Taylor, C. **Roads and Tracks of Britain,** 1979. JM Dent, London

Whittet, A. **The Bridleways of England,** Whittet Books, London

Wainwright, A. **Old Roads of Eastern Lakeland,** Westmorland Gazette, Kendal, 1985

Speakman, C and Abbott, S. **Great Walks from the Settle & Carlisle,** Leading Edge Press & Publishing, Hawes, 1987

Clayton, N. **Early Bicycles,** 1986. Shire Publications, Aylesbury

Watson W, and Gray, M. **The Penguin Book of the Bicycle,** Penguin Books, first published 1978

Ballantine, R. **Richard's Bicycle Book,** Pan Books, London, first published 1972 and revised several times since then

Matkin, R.B. **Map Reading,** Dalesman Publishing Co, Clapham, N Yorks.

Follow the Map, Ordnance Survey

Barry Ricketts, **The Mountain Biking Handbook,** The Arena Press, 1988

Pamphlets

Recreational Cycling in the Countryside, Countryside Commission Publications, 1989, CCP 259

Magazines

Lumley, P.R. **Mountain Bikes,** Footloose Magazine 16

Gabriel, T. **Riding the Steeps,** Outside Magazine, June 1986

Unknown, **Clunkers,** Bicycle Magazine, February 1983

Author (Iain Lynn), **Various,** Bicycle Times Magazine, 1984 - 1986

Fisher Cassie, W. **Pass-storming on a Jacobite Road,** CTC Gazette, May 1930

Other references and attributions will be found within the body of the text of this book

Publisher's Foreword

WHEN the first edition of our modest little ***Off-Road*** **Bicycle Book** appeared in November 1987, it represented an attempt to reflect the increasingly distinctive British dimension to an American 'fad'.

That cross-country cycling in Britain should have begun to evolve in its own direction was no surprise — after all, the dustry trails of California are a far cry from a Pennine peat bog in early spring.

The evolution of the British mountain bike scene — whose roots can equally be traced in a strong touring and cross-country tradition — had been keenly followed by the buoyant and enthusiastic cycling press. But the great majority of text books available at that time remained for some time solidly American, in both origin and content.

So **The *Off-Road* Bicycle Book** set out to redress the balance and reflect the British angle to the sport which presents the participant with such a wide choice: from the challenge of riding a bike where none have ridden before, or simply to potter with friends along pleasant byways in the knowledge that your bike will cope comfortably with gradients and obstacles. The first edition quickly sold out, and since then a number of 'all-British' books have followed in its wheel tracks. But this revised and updated version of **The *Off-Road* Bicycle Book** remains the only comprehensive volume on the market at a true 'pocket book' price.

Now, as then, our contributors are drawn from the ranks of those whose experience has helped shape the mountain bike scene in Britain — **Iain Lynn** joined the summit-baggers on the first bicycle ascent of Ben Nevis, while editor of the old *Bicycle Times*. **Richard Crane** bagged the rather bigger summit of Kilimanjaro, while his involvement with Intermediate Technology strengthens an ideological link between the simplicty of the bicycle as a machine and Third World development. **David Wrath-Sharman** and **Geoff Apps** were cycling cross-country well before the all-American (with Japanese components) mountain bike came on the scene. Indeed, had more notice been taken at the time, an all-British mountain bike might have evolved independently out of Geoff's design work.

To those whose contributions to the first edition are reproduced in this one, we add the name of **Tom Bogdanowicz**, who claims to have spent his infancy in a sidecar attached to a tandem. He now writes regularly about bicycles, whenever he is not working for a television news company. As the owner of a small fleet of bicycles — and a mountain tandem — he is well qualified as the compiler of the book's new section dealing with developments in the mountain bike market.

The publishers are again indebted to many in the industry for their help and patience and particular thanks are due to Ryedene Mountain Bikes, Two Wheels Good and the Keld Bike Centre in Swaledale. A full list of photographic credits appears overleaf.

Stan Abbott, Hawes, June 1989

List of illustrations

Chapter One

From Genesis to Revolution

LIKE so many great inventions from the wheel itself to penicillin, today's mountain bike owes its origins largely to an accident of history.

In 1933, a man by the name of Ignaz Schwinn produced a bicycle for children. It weighed 50 pounds, had huge balloon tyres and was almost unrideable. Yet his creation was destined to become the first real mountain bike.

That the modern, ultra lightweight and highly specialised mountain bike should have been spawned from such an inauspicious parent is in keeping with that fine tradition which dictates that events which change the shape of history often occur as a result of chance.

Schwinn based his design on observation; he looked around him, noted the style of motor cars of the period and modelled his bicycle on them. It had wide tyres, great sweeping handlebars and a broad seat. Later models even had false petrol tanks and lights built into the wide fenders (mudguards). The combination of their weight and balloon tyres meant they proved difficult to ride further than round the block.

Yet despite this, these machines became loved by a generation of American schoolkids and quickly became standard issue for anyone considering a newspaper round. They did nothing to encourage their young owners to take to the countryside for a few hours of relaxing cycling, of course, but they proved the ideal delivery machine. At this point, cycling was strictly kids' stuff. Car ownership was accelerating and the fabulous automobiles of the Thirties held the aspirations of millions of American parents.

The face of cycling began to change shortly after the Second World War, when Europe began to show the Americans what a real bicycle should look like. Small numbers of utility machines began to appear on the American market and these were vastly superior to the home-grown model. Almost all were considerably lighter and sported multiple gearing. Their tyres were much narrower and thanks to their lower rolling resistance and lighter weight, they could effectively burn off anything with an American headbadge. No wonder the Americans soon dubbed these bikes 'English Racers', even though they were about as pedestrian as you could imagine.

The revolution which the European machines heralded was shortlived, however; American business acumen being what it was, the home manufacturers soon started to produce cheaper, more shoddy copies and swamped the market with them. In time, what had started as a basically good design became diluted, and the English Racer at the hands of the

American manufacturer became a pale shadow of its former self.

During the great motoring boom of the Fifties, the humble bicycle was left pretty well in the doldrums and it wasn't until the ten-speed bicycle made its appearance during the Sixties that the situation began to change. Some of these machines were so expensive that they made cycling almost respectable again and their multiple gearing and narrow, quick tyres soon showed the American public that cycling need not always be hard work. Once again, the home manufacturer started to capitalise on the new bike's popularity. The result? Like the English Racer before it, the ten-speed degenerated into the ranks of garbage.

But this was not before the American public — and especially the American parent — discovered that cycling was a remarkably pleasant and efficient way of getting about. The humble bike was no longer a kid's toy. Ironically, it was the arrival of what **is** effectively a kids toy — the BMX bicycle — which was among events heralding the next stage in the genesis of the mountain bike.

In the Seventies BMX enabled kids to subject their bicycles to the utmost torture. They could go anywhere, do anything, and usually survive. Parents and older children could not fail to observe the fun these youngsters were having. Although the exact sequence of events is a little hazy, it is interesting that the sport which was ultimately to lead to the birth of the mountain bike was beginning to take off at around this time.

The sport in question involved steep mountainsides and motorcycles. The hillsides were tackled in a downwards direction, and at speed. Rough trails were raced over with gay abandon, perilously steep hillsides were fair game for anyone with a motorbike and nerve enough to try their luck. Youngsters would emulate their elders on old bicycles, no doubt dreaming of the day that they would be old enough to leap onto a motorcycle and join in properly.

Take a quiet mountainside, peaceful backwood trails, add more than a handful of exuberant motorcyclists and what do you get — trouble! The authorities did not like the idea of hordes of youngsters on motorbikes tearing around the countryside, ripping up the trails, disturbing the residents and generally proving a hazard to all and sundry. The problem was particularly acute in California and it was not long before the motorbikes were banned from trails and hillsides. Soon, the ban became more widespread. The new sport had died almost at birth.

Or had it? In no time, the adults were back on the hillsides, only this time on bicycles. They soon learnt that the best machines for careering down steep mountain sides were... the Schwinns. These proved the most durable and stable and the new devotees of the sport discovered that the Schwinn Excelsior, as produced between 1933 and the early 1940s, was the superior bike. The sport was forced to change slightly, thanks to the Schwinn's lack of gears and enormous weight. Riding it uphill was clearly out of the question, so pick-up trucks were pressed into service to get the riders and their machines up to the top.

It is at around this point, with the sport already more or less established in its crudest form, that certain key figures in the genesis of the mountain bike start to appear. The first of these is Gary Fisher, whose other claim to fame is as the course record holder in the so-called "Repack" race. The Repack was another of those peculiarly Californian customs and involved racing the Schwinn "clunkers" down a trail on Mount Tamalpais, dropping some 1,300ft in a little under two miles — an average gradient of about one-in-seven. It was so called because by the time the rider reached the bottom, all the grease in the old "coaster" brakes had turned to smoke and they had to be "repacked".

As a racing cyclist, Fisher was unac-customed to the Schwinn's lack of gearing. Moreover, he became bored with waiting at the bottom of the hill for hours for the pickup truck. The solution seemed simple enough — why not fit the Schwinn with gearing? He did so, enabling him to be first competitor not only to ride down the side of a hill but to ride back up again for the start of the next race. But his was not quite the first true mountain bike.

A framebuilder and long-standing track rival of Fisher's by the name of Joe Breeze had become interested and decided to take the Schwinn design one stage further. The machine was good for downhills but it was heavy and a little cumbersome and he was not convinced that it was its enormous weight which really made it the ideal mountain bike. Perhaps it was the frame dimensions and angles that made it so good in the dirt.

To test his theory, he copied the Schwinn dimensions but built them into a bike using lightweight tubing and components. The finished article weighed a lot less than 50lbs and his theory proved correct — the mountain bike, the true specialised lightweight off-road machine, had been born.

Joe Breeze had found a way of making the mountain bike (as it soon came to be called) lighter, better and more efficient than the Schwinns most people were using but it was still a very specialised machine and was for some time available only as a custom-built. Many riders willingly paid the kind of money one normally associates with the tailor-made machine.

Fisher joined forces with a one-time rock band roadie, Charlie Kelly, and then Tom Ritchey, a former member of the US national team, to form MountainBikes. American manufacturers had tooled up to produce bigger BMXs to cater for the kids as they grew up, but the anticipated adult BMX boom never happened and MountainBikes snapped up the parts.

In the early 80s they teamed up with top Japanese companies like Shimano and SunTour — the production all-terrain bike was born.

Mass production in a big way came when a man called Mike Sinyard showed interest in what was happening. His Specialized company sought to cater for the needs of cyclists not met elsewhere. He had a good nose for business and he commissioned a framebuilder to design him a machine which could be mass produced. He persuaded a Far East company to manufacture it, spent a fortune on advert-ising his new model and his Stumpjumper became an instant success.

The mountain bike was suddenly available to a far wider public and in the space of a few years there were few American or Japanese manufacturers without at least one mountain bike model in their range. But it would be two or three years before the mountain bike would make the trans-Atlantic leap to Britain.

The Challenge to Tradition

There has been a tradition of riding bicycles off the road in Britain and organisations like the Rough Stuff Fellowship can trace their history back to well before the Second World War. Yet off-road cycling never developed the way it did in America and perhaps it never would have done had it not been for the arrival of the American mountain bike in Britain.

Cycling in Britain reached its peak in the Twenties and Thirties, a time when the majority of the population was without any other personal transport. Equally, these were halcyon days for the cycling clubs, with thousands of people going out on a Sunday for the club run. This was an intensely social event and whole families took part. While cycling as a sport was involving many thousands of ordinary people, recreational touring was even more popular. Cycling was fun, social and entirely practical.

It was not long before some discovered that cycling along quiet country lanes was all well and good but pioneering tracks across the countryside was even more exciting. Rough stuff, as a derivitive of cycle touring, became an accepted part of touring generally, a pleasant non-competitive jaunt across the country, a chance to work up an appetite and admire the views from the hilltop.

As the years passed, bicycle technology advanced and machines became lighter, stronger and more reliable. Components became more sophisticated and the bicycles themselves got better and better. Yet at no point did anyone see any reason for the conventional touring bike to differ radically from the machine meant for rough stuff. The two were one and the same, though some rough stuff devotees

recognised the sense in strengthening key components or having frames specially built which would be a little stronger or make the bike a little easier to ride on rough tracks. Yet even these customisations differed little visibly from the standard touring machine on which they were based.

One of the very few exceptions to this rule was a machine called the Range Rider.

The Cleland Range Rider — before its time

This was designed during the late Seventies by Geoff Apps and, in many ways, was well ahead of its time. It used conventional tubing, though with a sloping top tube to increase the rider's mobility and a very much higher than normal bottom bracket. There was a special anti-bash plate protecting the triple chainset and wide, wide clearance between large diameter studded tyres and the forks and stays. It had a shorter wheelbase and steeper frame angles — all ideas which people said wouldn't catch on but which now reflect the direction taken by the industry.

During the late Seventies and early Eighties, the design was perfected, by which time it had become the Cleland Aventura. Yet the bike never really fired the imagination of the rough stuff cyclist. Not everybody took it seriously and a machine which was a very advanced

10

Rob Whittall has air to spare after clearing two cars — BMX was great fun until the bubble burst

Meanwhile, the merest sense of change began to infiltrate the British bike industry in the form of BMX. This tough little bike, the design of which had been pioneered in the United States, quickly became the schoolkid's most coveted possesion and it was not long before BMX bicycles began to flood into the country from America, the Far East, and Europe. Raleigh was arguably the first company to bring the BMX craze to Britain, in the form of the home-produced Raleigh Grifter, though British manufacturers had a very tough time competing with the overseas products, many of which were better marketed, better styled or better designed.

Sales of BMX bicycles went through the roof. Every kid wanted one. And within the space of three years, every kid seemed to have one. When the market became completed saturated and the BMX bubble finally burst, there were hundreds of companies, large and small, with great lorry loads of unwanted BMX machinery and rising debts. The craze was over and the industry in general was predictably cautious about messing with 'gimmicky' designs (as opposed to conventional roadsters) which might descend upon them from the land of crazes, the United States.

Enter the mountain bike. These extremely expensive, sophisticated and robust overgrown BMXs arrived in a market which was beginning to feel the pinch and the manufacturers, almost as one, called out 'Oh no, not again!' Such an unenthusiastic reception was understandable but it was only when people started to do things with these new-fangled machines that the manufacturers and the importers took notice. People cycled across the Sahara Desert, over mountains and along forest tracks on them and it was not long before the cycling press began to realise

mountain bike and which had, remarkably, evolved quite independent of the American design, became little more than an oddity. In the early days Jeremy Torr of English Cycles built bikes for Geoff — now, years later, the design has been developed by Dave-Wrath-Sharman whose Highpath is regarded by some as the most advanced off-road bike to date.

they were enormous fun and had lots of potential.

The major manufacturers, however, with the death knell of BMX ringing in their ears, decided to 'wait and see'. This left the way open for the Far East to get in and make the market its own. Ridgebacks, Muddy Foxes, Kuwaharas, Montanas and Specialized soon began to appear in the cycle dealer's window and, with the encouragement of enthusiastic media, the mountain bike began to sell.

Although most of the major manufacturers were dithering, the much smaller framebuilders saw the potential and started to experiment — it was easier for them as each machine was a virtual one-off and required little in the way of tooling up.

At first, suitable components were difficult to come by but that did not deter framebuilders from trying their hand. One of the first custom-built mountain bikes to emerge from a British workshop was a Dave Yates machine and although it was very much a prototype it worked extremely well. Bob Jackson, Chas Roberts and Billy Whitcomb were also on the scene early, exporting frames to the USA. Soon Jackson and other respected framebuilding names like FW Evans and Saracen began to offer mountain bikes to their customers. Some relied upon pure design genius (though many exchanged ideas between themselves in a way which would not happen in big industry), others looked to the lessons learnt during the BMX boom years. The result was a new breed of bicycle which was closely modelled on the American design but which remained essentially British.

The large manufacturers eventually got their act together though many were still a little unsure about it all until Raleigh finally unveiled their Mavericks.They

The Raleigh Maverick

were several years behind some of their competitors, with Dawes being one of the first of the large companies on the scene with its Ranger, but Raleigh's entry into the mountain bike market seemed to instil new confidence to the industry, with the result that virtually all of the major producers at the £200+ end of the cycle trade began to offer mountain bike models.

The mountain bike had finally arrived.

Tackling the Manx peak, Snaefell, on a Dawes Ranger

Chapter Two

Anatomy of the Mountain Bike

The Diamond Frame

BEFORE examining the mountain bike in detail, it is worth reflecting on the basic design bequeathed us by the cycle manufacturers of last century.

During the latter half of the 19th century, cycling enjoyed considerable growth in popularity. Bicycles came in all shapes and sizes, the most familiar of which is probably the Penny Farthing (or "Ordinary" as it is more correctly known). But there were many more designs which came and went, most of which did not quite enjoy the Ordinary's considerable popularity. Wheels could number anything from two to four, with the drive wheels situated to fore, aft or centrally, with the rider (or riders) sitting high, low, above the drive wheels, behind them, in between them or in almost any other position you could think of (and probably one or two you could not!).

The fundamental problem with these rather elegant and eccentric designs was that they were either cumbersome or difficult to ride and frequently both. The very idea of a young lady riding an Ordinary was quite preposterous, so this bicycle, the most efficient machine of the mid-Victorian era, was effectively off-limits to a great many people. In addition the considerable height of the Ordinary must have dissuaded many a male from embarking on a cycle ride along rutted,

A bike with a view — the Ordinary

country roads. It was not until Rover invented the Safety Bicycle that things improved.

If you look closely at a vintage Rover or Humber of the late 1880s, you will immediately be aware of its antiquity, but look again and you will see how remarkably similar it is to modern day bikes. The frame comprises two diamonds (roughly speaking) with the rear wheel at one end and the front wheel between a pair of forks at the other. There is a set of handlebars to steer by, a saddle to sit on, and it is the rear wheel which is driven —

An 1888 Rover Safety

not by means of cranks, levers or pedals bolted directly to the hub spindle — but by a chain and chainset. This last feature was one of the most significant innovations, in that one revolution of the wheel did not imply one revolution of the pedals or one stroke on the drive levers. Because the number of teeth on both the chainwheel and the rear sprocket could be altered, the gearing of the machine could be adjusted to suit the rider. The Safety was lighter, easier to ride, more approachable for novices and — thanks to its combination of sprocket, chain and chainwheel — more efficient.

Small wonder that — while materials have changed and manufacturing techniques improved — the basic design of the bicycle has altered little in over 100 years.

Frame Angles

So why is the diamond frame so good? Quite simply, it has proved to be the most ergonomically efficient (which means it is easy and comfortable to use). Comparatively simple and inexpensive to manufacture, above all it has proved immensely strong. Obviously, all these qualities should be fundamental features of a good mountain bike. But the technicalities of the diamond frame design are worth exploring to help explain why a mountain bike is designed the way it is.

Joe Breeze, the American framebuilder and off-road pioneer introduced in the last chapter knew what he was about when he decided to build a Schwinn copy out of modern lightweight materials. It was not the weight of the Schwinn which made it so acceptable but the overall design of the frame and particularly the frame angle configuration.

A cycle frame is constructed from a number of different tubes. Each is joined

to another by means of a lug (a sleeve of steel into which two tubes are butted together and brazed) or simply by brazing one against the other. This latter technique can be achieved in two ways — either by sticking one tube to another (crudely put, but this is essentially how chainstays are brazed to the seat tube directly below the saddle) or by building up quantities of bronze braze around the area of the join. This is most often seen on quality lugless frames where the join between two tubes is smooth and rounded. More recently, TIG (tungsten-inert gas) welding has been used, mainly on BMX frames though also on Muddy Fox mountain bikes. This is a welding technique in which the tubes are fused together with a metal filler rod by a high intensity electric arc within an inert gas shield to prevent oxidation — properly done it is very neat and clean. Messy welds are done by MIG (metal inert gas) technique.

The angle created between one tube and another has a fundamental effect on the ride characteristics of the the finished article. Good custom framebuilders will spend a good deal of time working out the angles between the tubes and it is important for the cyclist to understand why such care and attention is paid to them.

Let's identify the frame tubes first. The main diamond is made up of four tubes — seat tube, top tube, down tube and head tube. The seat tube is the one into which the saddle or seat pin is fitted and this leads down to the bottom bracket. From the top of the seat tube juts the top tube (and if you have slipped off the saddle of an over-sized bike as a child, you will have been painfully aware of its whereabouts!). From the bottom of the seat tube juts the down tube — normally where your bottle cage will

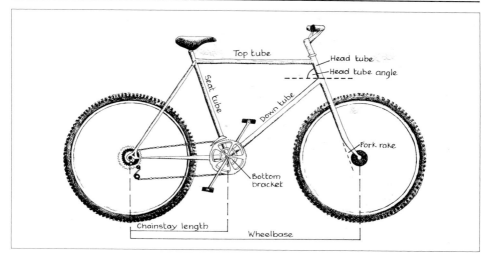

The naming of parts

be and, on a racer, your gear levers. Both the top tube and the down tube butt into the head tube, into which your handlebars are fitted.

The angles which are important are as follows. Firstly, the seat tube angle: this is the angle created by the lower edge of the top tube and the leading or forward edge of the seat tube. Quite why this is so important I will come to in a moment, after saying that the second most important is the head tube angle. To calculate this, place a protractor against the head tube,

ensuring that it is absolutely horizontal (use a spirit level). Line up the leading or rearward edge of the head tube with the centre spot of the protracter and take your reading. You can expect it to be between 69 and 73 degrees.

Of course, it isn't quite as easy as that — there are several other frame dimensions to consider, but we'll come to those in a moment.

The head angle dictates the way the steering will perform. For example, on a racing bike it will probably be about 74

Varying fork rakes on mountain and racing bikes

15

degrees (remember that 90 degrees is absolutely vertical) and this will make the steering of the bike suitably racy — very quick and very responsive, a little twitchy even. On a touring bike, the head angle is more likely to be around 72 degrees, making the steering slightly less responsive but a little more preditcable and comfortable.

These dimensions must also be related to the fork rake. To understand what this is, draw a line straight down the centre of the front fork blades to the ground. You will notice that the fork blade is bent forward at the bottom and the wheel is visibly forward of your line. The distance from the line to the hub spindle will show you how far the fork blade is offset — the fork rake. This also has a marked affect on the ride characteristics of your bike. A shallow fork rake (less than 50mm) will make the steering and handling of the bike very quick and twitchy and this is the usual racing set-up. On a touring bike, the fork rake is normally greater, making the steering more stable and helping to iron out bumps and potholes. A combination of shallow head angle (72 degrees) and short fork rake is disastrous and the reverse is also true. In practice, you rarely find a bike built like this.

So the shallower the head angle and the longer the fork rake, the more relaxed and more stable the ride. The steeper the head angle and the shorter the fork rake, the bumpier, less stable — but more responsive — the ride. Right. Now the seat angle.

This is merely another way of saying how far behind the bottom bracket the rider is sitting. This too can have a marked effect on the ride characteristics of a bicycle. For example, a racing cyclist wanting to apply explosive power to the pedals will want to be sitting almost directly above them, so

the seat angle will typically be around 74 or 75 degrees — quite steep. On a touring bike this is less important so the angle will be around 72 degrees, which makes for a slightly more relaxed riding position.

These are the principle dimensions to consider when discussing a frame's performance or suitablity. Before using this information to analyse the mountain bike, let us consider one final dimension — the rear triangle.

The chain stays jut out of the back of the bottom bracket to the rear of the bike and run parallel to the chain. They join forces with the seat stays directly above the rear wheel spindle. The chain stay length is the distance from the bottom bracket axle to the rear dropout or hub axle.

The simple rule is, the shorter the wheelbase, the more agile the bike — but the harsher the ride, especially over rough ground. Conversely, the longer the wheelbase, the less agile the bike but it will be easier and more comfortable to use on rough terrain. And bikes with short chain stays (and hence probably short wheelbases) are generally better hill climbers. This is because the shorter the chain stays, the more weight there is on the back wheel, and hence the more traction available.

Frame design and the mountain bike

Now to the mountain bike. The standard design inherited from the Americans will typically have a head angle of 69 degrees or so. This makes the steering extremely stable and comfortable, enabling the machine to remain controllable over even the roughest of ground. An angle any steeper than this will make the steering buck wildly and the bike will be less controllable. The seat angle, too, will be around 69 degrees, thus placing the rider well back over the rear of the bike with the pedals well forward. The effect these two angles have, therefore, is to make the mountain bike perform quite sluggishly on the road (certainly when compared to a racer) but this sluggishness is transformed into stability as soon as you leave the road and hit the dirt.

There are two other major features to consider. Because the seat tube is comparatively 'laid back' it is in danger of scraping against the back tyre, so the rear wheel must be kept well away from it by making the chainstays fairly long. The same thing is happening at the front of the bike, too. Because the head angle is so shallow the fork rake must be correspondingly generous and these two factors push the front wheel well forward of the handlebars. So with the front wheel well out in front and the rear wheel well aft of the pedals, the common-or-garden 'first generation'[1] mountain bike will have a pretty long wheelbase.

But didn't we say that a short wheelbase makes for better hill climbing? That's right, so you can deduce from all of this that the mountain bike is a pretty lousy hill climber. Technically this is true, but the very low gearing common to good mountain bikes obviously helps to counteract this. But in all honesty, because the rider's weight can seldom be directly over the rear wheel, mountain bikes can suffer from a certain loss of traction on steep slippery slopes. Not ideal, perhaps, and there are framebuilders offering custom-made ATBs with a shorter than normal wheelbase to improve the uphill performance and this trend is reflected in second and third generation machines.

But there are compensations with this design. The sheer length of the bikes's wheelbase increases its stability over rough ground and makes it more comfortable to ride. Take a trip along an undulating backroad in a limousine and then try the same trip in a Mini and you will see how a long wheelbase helps to iron out the bumps.

The second feature you might notice about an ATB is that the pedals are a long way off the ground. This is because the bottom bracket is higher than on sports machines — and it needs to be. Take a ride across a boulder field or through rough heather and you will want your delicate chainset to be as far away from the ground as possible. This also helps prevent the bike from 'grounding' on bumps.

You might also notice that the frame tubing is fairly chunky, or at least of a greater diameter than tubes made into touring or racing bikes. This is to make the ATB stronger but, of course, it isn't as simple as that.

Whole chapters have been written about frame tubing, stress mechanics and the like but I don't intend to delve too deeply into the technicalities as it can all become a little esoteric, not to say tedious. In short, frame tubing is made not from plain steel but from steel alloys — steel with quantities of chromium, molybdenum, manganese and other elements. This imparts varous qualities to the steel, making it lighter, stronger, stiffer, easier to braze or more resilient in the face of relentless pounding. The best ATBs will have little stickers saying 'Made from Chro-Mo tubing' or Reynolds 531 (or 501), Columbus, Tange, Vitus, Ishiwata. British custom builders seem to prefer Columbus, the Americans, Tange Prestige, while the Canondale uses very wide diameter aluminium alloy tube.

Components

So much for the frame. Now for the hardware. You can expect your ATB to have something like 15 gears, often as many as 18. The latter is derived from having a freewheel with six sprockets connected via a chain to a triple chainset fitted with three different sizes of chainring (3 x 6 = 18). The former will have only a five-speed block connected to the same chainset (3 x 5 = 15). The gears themselves will be pitched pretty low to enable you to climb slopes steeper than you might care to imagine. You can expect pretty large steps between one gear and the next — this is to give you a range of gears which will have you flying along a country road one moment and climbing lamp posts the next.

The kind of derailleur gear fitted to a mountain bike is not radically different to look at from one which would be fitted to a touring machine. It will appear more elongated to cope with the vast length of excess chain left over when you are on the smallest chainring and a small freewheel sprocket but it will still allow the chain onto the largest chainring and a large sprocket. So the gear cage length (the distance between the uppermost jockey wheel and the lower one) will be considerable. If you compare wide ratio gear mechs like these, you might also notice that the ATB version is chunkier and looks pretty robust. The front mechanism — the one which changes the chain from one ring to the next — will often look fairly standard though in fact the cage through which the chain passes will often be a little deeper than normal.

Nearly all the latest bikes have Shimano SIS or SunTour Acushift gears, giving rise to the popular acronym,'Acusis'.

All or most bearings will be sealed — this is to keep grease in and manufacturers will make no claims that they will keep all water out.

The handlebars will be pretty wide too and you can expect a choice of two designs. The Bullmoose, Ritchey or Mooseneck is usually made from steel or a steel alloy and forms a diamond shape directly above the headset so this is a one-piece design. The Slingshot, or swan-neck, has a separate (usually alloy) handlebar stem through which is threaded an alloy handlebar, usually curved, allowing some adjustment, unlike the Bullmoose-style which is welded together and is now less popular as it has to be custom made for comfort.

Above — Bullmoose-style bars on a Shimano Ridgeback, and — below — the Slingshot version

Onto the handlebars will be mounted a pair of brake levers which will probably look similar to motorcycle levers. Believe me, the design works, especially on steep descents.The brakes themselves are usually cantilever operated and extremely powerful.

Also on the handlebars will be a pair of thumbshifter gear levers. Nobody wants to take their hands off the steering to change gear while negotiating tricky terrain.

Perhaps the most conspicuous feature of a mountain bike is its tyres. These are usually huge knobbly affairs designed for optimum off-road traction when the going gets slippery. They are generally fitted to two types of rim, 32mm and 28mm. The 2.125-inch tyre is the standard off-road model gnerally found on first and second generation machines and looks like it'd be more at home on a LandRover. Narrower tyres are quicker and more suited to city riding and range from 1.5-inch to 1.9-inch, although some third generation mountain bikes opt for narrower tyres as they can offer better grip through their higher running pressure.

The tyres themselves can come in a variety of designs. For the true off-road bike you will probably find yourself with a tyre which is covered in knobs and protrusions. These make a humming noise on tarmac and can feel sluggish, but they really come into their own off the road. At the other extreme you have the narrow tyre designed for narrow rims, sometimes with a pronounced ridge down the centre. These are great for road use but not so good for rough riding. A compromise is the 2.125 tyre with a central ridge, combining the narrow central ridge for road use and plenty of tread for off-road work. Many ATBs come fitted with this as standard, but they should be used at higher inflation on-road than off.

A different philosophy is employed by Highpath and Cleland who use Finnish Hakka tyres on big 650B tandem rims

Mitsuboshi tyres ranging from, left, a 1.75-inch city bike Cruiser model to the Grippa ATB tyre

(mountain bikes normally use 650Cs). The rims are only 22mm, but the tyres are up to 2-inch and even come in studded versions for winter. The tyres have eevolved to cope with Scandinavian dirt roads and the larger diameter wheel means lower rolling resistance.

You might also notice that your ATB has a quick-release mechanism fitted instead of a seat binder bolt. This enables you to adjust the height of the saddle in a trice and can be very useful (more of that in Chapter 3). Some machines also come fitted with frame pads. These are usually located at the join between the top and seat tubes directly under the saddle and are designed to make carrying the bike over rivers and stiles a little more comfortable.

The riding position on a mountain bike is fairly upright and this means that the points of contact between you and the bike have to be well designed. As the larger portion of your body weight will be borne on the saddle (more so than on a tourer), you should at least have an anatomic saddle with special padding directly below the pelvis. Sprung saddles with coil springs fitted to the rear are even better. Best of all is a sprung leather saddle though this will take some time to 'break in', eventually conforming exactly to the shape of your rump (see Chapter Four). Pedals are usually fairly substantial affairs, either broad flat Platform pedals or jagged Beartraps, both of which are designed to accommodate boots or large shoes.

The mountain bike sounds quite a complicated and specialised machine and in one sense it is. However, all the components are fairly standard to all high quality bicycles, albeit with slight design changes to make then more suitable to the work which a mountain bike will enjoy. And for all they might sound horrendously difficult to get to grips with, riding them is simplicity itself.

Well....

[1] *The terms first, second and third generation as used in this book require some definition.'First generation' mountain bikes have their roots in the basic Scwinn design, featuring long wheelbase, long chainstays, low bottom bracket and very laid back seat and steering angles (68° parallel). This covers bikes up to about 1984 (Dawes Ranger).*

Second generation machines often emply the same angles, but have shorter chainstays, slightly shorter wheelbase, but much higher bottom bracket (Overbury Pioneer).

Third generation covers designs from 1987 on, exhibiting steeper frame angles (70°) and high bottom bracket and—most importantly—higher handle bars and a more upright riding position. The upmarket Cannondale SM600-SM900 series is a good example.

Chapter Three

Riding Technique and the Three Bs

THE mountain bike is one of the most approachable of bicycles — the frame geometry and the type of componentry combine to produce a machine which is basically very easy to ride. Both factors dictate the riding position — and on a mountain bike it is this perhaps more than anything else which inspires confidence and a sense of adventure.

If you compare the respective riding positions of a mountain bike and a common-or-garden sports bike, you will notice that they are significantly different. The geometry of the sports racer encourages the rider to lean forward onto the dropped handlebars and in extreme cases the back can be almost parallel to the top tube. The rider, therefore, adopts an aerodynamic position and it is precisely because of this stretched out, forward leaning position that racing cyclists can often be quite happy and comfortable using the narrowest of narrow saddles. Because of the steep seat tube, the saddle is almost directly above the bottom bracket so the rider must be able to thrust downwards with the legs without his or her thighs chafing on the side of the saddle.

The same cannot be said of the mountain bike, whose rider adopts a much more upright position, head high and body well behind the bottom bracket. Because of this upright posture, the body's weight will be more concentrated on the saddle, so this must needs be broader and more support-ive. The sheer width of the handlebars also helps the rider to adopt a broad stance and this in turn enables the exertion of great leverage over the steering. Mention must also be made of the frame geometry. Because of the shallow head angle the bike will naturally want to travel in a straight line (it is very easy to ride 'hands off' for this reason) and this combined with the broad handlebars makes for a very stable and easy machine to ride.

However, it is important that the riding position is finely tuned for you. This involves getting the height of handlebars and saddle right.

Let's start with the saddle. For ordinary road conditions you need to have your saddle high enough for leg to be extended as far as you feel is safe — 1.1 x your inside leg measurement from pedal to saddle is a proven rule. Being able to touch the ground while sitting on the saddle is not essential — move off the saddle when you stop.

The best way to obtain the optimum saddle height is to sit on the saddle and lean against the garage door or garden fence. Place the ball of your right foot on the pedal and rotate until it is in the 6 o'clock position. If your leg is now almost straight (almost, remember) then you should have the saddle height about right. Because of the comparatively high bottom bracket, you will not be able to get both your feet flat on the ground but you ought to be able to balance on your toes and that is good enough. Tests have shown that if you have the saddle too low it can cost 30 per cent of your power — too high and you could lose five per cent.

There are no hard and fast rules governing your handlebar position. Use a spanner to adjust the height until you achieve a comfortable and relaxed position. This can mean different things to different people so take a little while to experiment to see what works for you. If your bike has an alloy stem with a set of curved handlebars passing through it you will also be able to loosen the clamp and swivel the bars. In this way you can have the bars upswept, downswept, swept forward or back. Find out which position feels most comfortable. You will have slightly less in the way of positional choice with Bullmoose-style bars.

The brake levers should fall readily to hand, as should the thumbshifters. You can adjust their position though this is better done after you have been riding the bike for a while — the most comfortable position may not be obvious immediately.

Triple chainsets look horrendously complicated if you are not used to them but I guarantee that within 30 minutes of using one you will be wondering what all the fuss was about. You will find the thumbshifters easy to use and if you already ride a bike then you will love the way you don't have to take your hands off the steering to make a gear change. Usually (but not always) you have to push against the ratchet to change onto a bigger

cog or sprocket and sometimes you have to adjust the grub nuts a little to make the gear mechanism achieve slick changes every time. In particular, changing down onto the smallest chainring can be a little hit-or-miss, especially if the chain is worn. Practise your gear changes, get used to the way they feel and ease off on the pedals slightly while you change from one cog or chainring to another. In time, you will learn to anticipate gear changes and hit the right gear smoothly every time.

Basic Skills

Once you become used to changing gear and generally feel familiar with the way the bike performs, it is time to get down to some real off-road work. Most of the time, the bike will behave off-road in almost exactly the way it does on the road — although it will feel bumpier! But forest tracks will feel like tarmac and all you have to do is ride. Watch out for loose gravel on the bends, though: corner too fast on the loose stuff and you might find yourself in the trees.

Steep ascents require some basic technique. To obtain maximum power through the pedals, you will want to be far forward on the saddle (and more directly above the bottom bracket) and have the saddle high up. Try to keep your torso vertical too. For long downhills — just like the ones we don't have many of in the UK — you can let the saddle down a bit.

Unfortunately, keeping your torso vertical also means that your body weight is well forward of the rear driving wheel. On loose or slippery ground, this can mean that the rear wheel loses traction and 'spins out'. On a long ascent, this can become really, really b-o-r-i-n-g. Getting up off the saddle and sticking your butt out and up in the air helps to keep the weight over the back though obviously this is a little more tiring than simply sitting down and pedalling. Try mixing it — off the saddle for a while, back in the saddle for a breather, out of the saddle again, and so on.

Of course, downhills are what the mountain bike was all about in the first place and for many people they are still the high point of a day out on the hills. Steep descents can be either exhilarating or terrifying. The former is preferable in most cases, the latter easily avoided if you get your technique right and slow down.

The only way to stay in control of your machine is by using the **brakes** — the first of the **three Bs**. The brakes are essentially a means of control, that is, staying on the bike. With these you can control your descent, decelerate, allow the bike to accelerate and dictate the speed and the way the bike approaches an obstacle or travels over a section of difficult terrain. Remember that cantilever brakes can be pretty forceful so use with discretion. Most of your braking should be done with the rear brake and you should use this to control your speed — that is, maintaining a steady rate of decent, gently slowing yourself down, allowing the machine to go a little faster, and so on. You might find that you have the rear brake on nearly all the time. Don't worry about it. This is par for the course.

If you need to apply the brakes a little more firmly, then use the front. This will slow you down quite quickly, so use it gently. Don't hang on to the front brake or you will probably beat your bike to the bottom of the hill and batter your knees against the handlebars into the bargain. This is called the face plant and usually involves being launched over the top of the bars and landing on your head.

There is one other point worth bearing in mind when you use the front brake. If you have it on quite firmly on a very steep but controlled descent, you may find that something rather surprising happens when you hit a bump, a ridge or a log. The front wheel locks up and you start pirouetting — the beginnings of a slow motion face plant. This happens because the resistance being applied to the rim plus the added resistance against the wheel when it encounters an obstacle all combine to make the brakes work even better — and suddenly, even better. So if you see a log, a high bump or a rock approaching, ease off on the front wheel and allow the momentum of the bike to carry you over.

While all this is happening, your best **body** position is one which looks a trifle silly — with your butt almost trailing against the rear wheel. The trick here is to stretch yourself back over the rear of the saddle and as low down as possible, legs braced against the pedals, arms absolutley straight. Tuck your thighs under the saddle, it will give you something else to brace against. More often than not, you will be content just to drop the saddle as far as it can go and sit it all out in luxury, though it is worth practising the bum scraping position in case things become a little more serious than you first anticipated. Don't they always?

As you will have gathered, sitting well back and low over the back wheel is best for downhills and almost all good mountain bikes are fitted with quick-release clamps so you can drop the saddle and adopt the position in relative comfort. The reverse, as we have said, is true on long uphills where you want to keep your weight well forward to apply maximum power.

Now for the final of the three Bs which

are essential in technically good mountain biking — **balance**. Like braking and body position, this is important whether you ride uphill, downhill, or on the flat, especially when the going gets rough.

Balance is just as important as braking. Bicycles have a tendency to fall over, because they have only two wheels and most are not fitted with stabilisers. However, when you learn to ride a bicycle, you learn to stay upright by steering into a fall. If the bike starts to fall to the left, you simply steer to the left and the bike rights itself. Simple, and it soon becomes second nature.

However, on a mountain bike, it might not always be possible to steer yourself out of a fall. Obviously, if you are sitting in the saddle then you will only really be able to steer by using the handlebars. This will enable you to steer out of a sideways fall but only on smooth ground. On rougher ground, you might find yourself having to do two things at once — keeping upright and steering your way around bumps, rocks and ridges. The two often conflict — your sense of balance says steer to the left, the terrain says steer to the right. The result can be a moment's indecision and a messy spill.

Over particularly rough or rocky ground, I find that standing on the pedals means I can change the position of my body very quickly. You can achieve perfect balance and retain control over your direction either by using your body as a counterbalance by leaning right out to the side, or by leaning the bike over while keeping your body upright. Standing up in the pedals makes the whole machine more nimble and manoeuverable and the body's innate sense of balance will usually take over when the going gets tough.

Advanced Riding Techniques

Developing the use of body positions is the next stage — to dictate not simply whether the bike stays upright but how efficiently it performs in any given circumstance.

For example, you are riding along a rough mountain track and you encounter a stream running across your path. The stream is not very deep, but it is a little rocky and the groove it has cut is fairly deep. Put your front wheel in there and it will stop dead rather than climb out the

Jamie Carr pops a wheelie over a log

other side. What do you do? Or you are riding along the same mountain track and you come across a 6" rocky step. If you ride straight at it you might get the front wheel up but the jarring through the front forks and handlebars will be sickening. You might also damage the forks, the fork crown, the steering column, the wheel rim and the tyre, not to mention your arms. Should you get off?

The answer to both of these questions is to 'pop a wheelie', as they say. This involves throwing your body right back over the rear wheel and pulling hard on the handlebars to physically lift the front wheel off the ground and over the obstruction. This can be done either sitting on the saddle or standing on the pedals. The heave on the handlebars should also pull you up into a standing position and this is desirable on two counts. Firstly, it will mean that your legs will absorb the thumb from the rear wheel as it hits the obstruction your front wheel has just neatly avoided. Secondly, it places you right above the pedals in a position of maximum thrust, enabling you to power the rear wheel either out of the deep rivulet or over the edge of the step.

This is quite a simple but a most effective technique and can be used in a variety of circumstances. There may be occasions when you do not actually need to lift the front wheel off the ground at all, but merely lighten it slightly. You can do this either by placing your body not quite so far back, not pulling quite so hard on the handlebars or a combination of both. Remember that most mountain bikes have a fairly long wheelbase and are therefore difficult to stand on their back wheels. Of course, it is always possible to pull your bike over backwards, but you would have to be trying damned hard!

Using fine control to get out of trouble on a descent

Bunny hops are the next stage on and much more difficult. This involves lifting the front wheel up in the air and then immediately lifting the back wheel off the ground so that you are airborne. Impossible? Not quite.

Pop a wheelie in the usual fashion. As soon as the front wheel rears up, transfer your weight from the rear of the bike to the front — and **HARD!** This throws the front wheel down and the bike pivots in mid air, thus lifting the rear wheel off the ground. Well, that's the theory, anyway. It takes quite a bit of practice to get it right every time and while the bunny hop might not be the most useful of riding techniques, it looks impressive and is great fun! So who says mountain biking has to be serious all the time?

A front wheel pivot is one method when — on a particularly tortuous descent — you decide you want to go across the slope rather than straight down.

You will already be hanging well over the back wheel, or at least you ought to be. The back wheel will probably be locked on tight, with the front brake half-on to control your rate of descent. This is where the fun starts. Lock the front wheel with the front brake and move your weight forward slightly. This is a surefire way of doing a face plant but hopefully it won't go quite that far! You are now balancing on the front wheel and, no doubt, panicking like crazy.

Once you have the back wheel off the ground, shift your body weight sideways a little. This will bring the back wheel around in the direction you are leaning (still off the ground, remember). Once this begins to happen, lean the other way to maintain your balance. When the back wheel has come round as far as it you want it, release the front brake a little and the back wheel will come back to earth (usually quite firmly). As you release the brake, straighten up the handlebars. You have now changed your direction of travel.

It sounds quite simple, but be warned — it is not easy, and if it goes wrong in the

Oh, my god !

Balancing on the front wheel panicking like crazy....

wrong place you could be taking a helicopter ride to hospital.

A safer way out of the same situation is to take a leftwards descent across the slope, the left being the side most people are used to getting off the bike on. You can let the bike slide, wheels locked, with your knee out at right angles, ready to 'bale out' and let go of the bike if needs be. But even this is best only used for, say, dropping into a gully where you know you won't have far to fall.

The rear wheel slide looks even more impressive but is anti-social because it really carves up the ground and should be used only as a last desperate resort.

Imagine yourself hurtling down a forestry track. You suddenly, and at the last moment, realise that the bend ahead is much, much tighter than you anticipated and there is a five bar gate across your path into the bargain. What do you do, (apart from panic)?

Your first response will almost certainly be to lock up the back wheel and hang pretty hard on the front, too. This will give you a straight line skid, which is pretty ineffectual. You're still going to hit the gate or go off the track into the trees. But if you try flicking the back end out (steering one way and then immediately the other) just before you hit the brakes, you will go into a sideways slide. This should always be a controlled slide and you can control it by steering into the slide, which will have the effect of straightening the bike up again, but not so much that it will pull out and head for the gate again.

If you throw the back end of the bike out to the right, then your left foot should be off the pedal and dragging along the ground. This will help you to stay more or less upright and increase your braking (two brakes and a foot, right?). The bike will naturally veer off to the side so if the coast is clear you can probably release the brake once you feel confident the bike is under control again, and end up riding parallel to the gate.

But be warned. Few people can get themselves into a fast sideways slide and come out of it in the upright position. It takes a lot of practice to get the combination of slide, steering and braking right and you are more than likely to end up on the floor. This might not be terribly comfortable but it beats the hell out of hitting a gate at 25 miles per hour. It is a technique worth practising just in case you find yourself in a tight spot sometime, but for goodness sake don't tell anyone I told you! Like I said, this will really carve the track up. Don't be anti-social about it — it could ruin it for everyone.

You can't really talk about riding technique without mentioning the fact that, someday, you are going to have to carry your bike. This is often unavoidable, especially if you enjoy going high into the mountains or well off the beaten track.

There are two ways of doing this. The first is used for fairly short spells, like crossing fences, stiles or rivers. Simply put your arm through the main diamond and throw the bike up on your shoulder. The top tube will be running down the front of your body, the seat tube down the back, so that the saddle is almost resting on the side of your head. Let's say that you are carrying the bike on your right shoulder. You should find that you can reach the handlebars with your right hand. Do so, and hold the bars about 6" to the right of the headset. This will hold the bike where it is and keep the front wheel from bashing you in the knees. The technique becomes uncomfortable after a while, so frame pads will help.

Carrying the bike — a carry strap helps

The other way is to carry the whole bike around your neck. To do this, stick your head through the main diamond and throw the bike up so that the seat tube is resting and running across the back of your shoulders. Be careful that the chainset does not stick in your neck as this can hurt rather a lot — guess where your jugular vein runs. For the same reason, always carry the bike so that the chainset is over your **right** shoulder, never your left (guess where your jugular vein runs).

Once again, some form of padding will aid comfort and this is dealt with the next chapter. In the meantime, suffice to say that this is the most comfortable way to carry a mountain bike for prolonged spells.

27

Above — getting away from it all and, left, a technique for longer carries

Chapter Four

Accessories

THE mountain bike is, by nature, a fairly simple beast. Wheels, transmission, brakes, something to sit on, something to steer with and that's about it. All these you should find on the bike when you buy it.

However, there are numerous accessories you can fit to make your hours awheel just that little bit more enjoyable or convenient. Most of these are hardly specialised and can be just as much at home on a touring bicycle, though there are a number of accessories which are made specifically for the mountain bike user. Those which aren't need to be selected with care, as they are almost certain to receive more wear and tear on a mountain bike than they will on a tourer.

Simple Add-ons

One of the simplest and most useful accessories is a set of frame pads. If you are lucky, then these will already be fitted when you buy your bike. These are merely strips of closed cell foam which have been moulded so they wrap around the frame tubes underneath the saddle, where the top and seat tubes intersect. They are usually covered in a tough cordura nylon for durability and washability, this cover also helping to hold the foam pads in place, usually with Velcro strips.

Such a hard, unyeilding and heavy object balanced on an area where the bones are fairly close to the surface of the skin is guaranteed to make your shoulder sore — frame pads help to spread the weight of the

bike a little more evenly and make carrying the machine a far less painful process.

Muddy Fox have their own frame pads and these are fitted to some of their machines and offered as accessories for the others. Most other manufacturers fit frame pads to their top models and these are also available through your specialist lightweight cycle shop as add-ons.

A bash bar is another very good idea. These bolt on to the rear drop-out (this usually means you having to remove the gear mechanism, placing the bar against the drop-out and then re-bolting the gear mech in place over the top of it). The bash bar hangs out over the top of and down over the gear mech and thus protects it from rocks or falls. Gear mechs are fairly

Bash bars and plates to protect vulnerable mechanisms

delicate so it pays to look after them at the cost of a small weight and financial penalty.

An increasing number of mountain bikes come ready fitted with bottle cage bosses, enabling you to bolt a bottle cage directly onto the frame. Bottle cages can also be bolted to a frame with clips. The strongest bottle cage I have seen originates from a small company in Macclesfield called Nimrod Products. This is made from alloy, but the alloy rod from which it is formed is a great deal thicker than that used in most other alloy cages. It is therefore extremely strong and such strength is well worth having, especially on a mountain bike.

The bottles themselves are fairly standard and pretty inexpensive. As yet, no-one has found a reason for inventing a special mountain bike bottle but I have no doubt that it is only a question of time.

Improving your specification

Some people find that their mountain bike is just a little too basic for their needs and the most frequent addition to the basic specification is a rack — something to hang panniers on or strap items of clothing or small bags to.

In recent years a profusion of alloy racks has hit the market and now few top quality touring bikes will be seen dead with anything else. The Blackburn racks were the first in Britain and are still, to my mind, the best, but racks from Tonard, Allez, and Karrimor are all pretty good and probably just as strong.

What a mountain biker is looking for is a rack which is good and strong and that usually means four-point fixing. Most racks, alloy or steel, are bolted to a special brazed-on 'eye' above each of the two rear drop-outs. On a three-point fixing rack,

Four-point fixing rack

there is also an (often) adjustable strut which bolts between the rear brake and the bridge to which it is fitted. That means that the rack is bolted to three anchor points — two drop-outs and the brake bridge.

The four-point fixing rack does away with this adjustable strut and has two separate struts instead. These are bolted to the seat stays, either directly into special bosses or with the aid of clips and bolts. Because there are two anchor points here, several inches apart, this considerably reduces a loaded rack's habit of swaying from side to side.

Most people are quite happy with the saddle their bike comes with. Many will be Anatomics-style, with special padding beneath the pelvic bones to prevent soreness around these two pressure points. Because of a rider's relatively upright posture, the saddle needs to be fairly broad and this will also help make it more comfortable.

Names to look for if you want a better seat include the Madison G11 and the superior Madison G12, the latter having a special hydro-elastic gel which conforms to the shape of your pelvis and performs

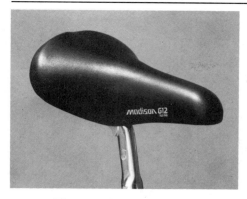

The superior Madison G12

slightly better than the usual foam padding.

Then there's the good old-fashioned Brooks leather saddle. These are as hard as iron to begin with but, once treated with a leather softener (Mars oil, Neatsfoot oil, Brooks Proofhide or similar) they become much more pliable and actually conform to the exact shape of your rump. In a short time the saddle will fit perfectly — and will fit nobody else! Now, that's comfort!

For ATB use, choose the B66 Champion which is the B17 touring saddle on springs. It is much broader and the mattrass springs at the back make it ideal for crossing rough ground. Though I personally have a soft spot for Brooks, other leather saddles from companies such as Lepper or Ideale will probably serve just as well, if you can find them.

As I mentioned in the last chapter, you usually need to change your position on the saddle depending on whether you are riding uphill or downhill — well forward for ascending, well back for descending. This usually means either hanging off the back of the saddle or sitting right on the prow, neither position being particularly comfortable.

However, the SR ATB seat pillar helps to improve this situation slightly by enabling the saddle to be moved fore and aft. A simple quick-release lever on the underside allows the whole saddle and saddle clamp assembly to slide along a 'track' by some 3" — without altering the horizontal pitch of the saddle at all. This is great for really long ascents or descents, but it becomes a bit of a pain if you have to stop and re-adjust it every five minutes — a nice idea but you might find it becomes superfluous.

Some riders might be able to make a case for mudguards, particularly if the bike is going to be used both off-road and on-road — indeed, many would argue that mudguards are a must in cold, wet weather, particularly if you are riding in a group, and that aspiring to a macho image is no good reason for going without.

Until the cycle accessory company Bluemels crashed in 1985, the standard had been set by its Mountain Guard, a tough, very wide section chromoplastic mudguard with galvanised steel stays. The company and all its machinery were bought by SKS of Germany and for some time the Mountain Guard was not available.

With Mountain Guards now back on the market, other British companies including Spencer Manufacturing of Tenbury Wells and SPD Accessories, a company consisting largely of the old Bluemels workforce, are producing similar products

Beast of Burden

You can always find a place for luggage on a bike. You might need to carry tools, the odd spare, sandwiches and waterproofs so it might as well be a piece of luggage which fits to the bike rather than the body. See also next chapter.

Needless to say, the two major names in the cycle luggage market, Carradice and Karrimor, have been the first to apply their thoughts to the mountain bike user. Karrimor led the way with their Kalahari range of luggage, initially front panniers, rear panniers and a rear pannier which converts into a rucksack. They have since added other luggage ideas in the Kalahari vein. Carradice arrived a little late with the Prima, a small front or rear rucksack convertible pannier.

Karrimor's Kalahari luggage is constructed from tough 1000 denier KS100e, Karrimor's own nylon-based fabric. The panniers are broader than their

Karrimor Kalahari luggage being put through its paces

on-road stablemates and not quite as deep. This raises the centre of gravity slightly but gives improved clearance on rough,

heathery or rocky ground. Extremely well designed, these panniers are also very tough, though the rucksack pannier (the Mountain) can become a little painful to carry after a few hours and does not compare altogether favourably with a real rucksack. But the fact that it can be carried either on the bike or on the back is a substantial bonus.

Carradice's offering is typical Carradice — simple, efficient and almost totally indestructible. This, the Prima, is made from tough Cordura and cotton duck and is clearly built to last. Its size makes it suitable as either a front or rear pannier and it has been designed so that two panniers can be joined together base to base, making one large backpack.

You might think that something as simple as luggage would be free from con- troversy, but you'd be wrong....thinking has been shifting and off-road aficionados now reckon that panniers, while fine for touring and pottering, are not the best bet for serious all-terrain work, the thesis being that for maximum stability, the weight should move with the rider and not with the bike.

Recommended are light rucksacks like the Karrimor Vista range. For short trips a bum bag or hip sack — what the Americans call a 'fanny pack' — fitted to a belt is a good bet and comes from Tailwind, Muddy Fox or Berghaus.One company was, at the time of writing, working on an extending bum bag system to solve all problems for the serious ATB person.

Virtually any other item of cycle luggage designed for the touring cyclist will fit on a mountain bike, though handlebar bags can be a problem to fit because of the design of some ATB bars, making the fitment of a barbag support almost impossible. Bags which don't need a special support include the Karrimor Bardet and Karrimor have been nice enough to offer this item in Kalahari colours for that co-ordinated look. It is also, quite sensibly, in Kalahari fabric — 1000 denier KS100e.

A small bag has also been developed to fit over the triangle on a set of mooseneck bars. This first made its appearance on top flight Muddy Fox machines and Karrimor have followed this up by producing the same small zipped pouch as part of the Kalahari range. It's not very big, of course, but you might find it useful for keys, a small camera and personal equipment.

Headgear

If you will be using your mountain bike at all seriously then a helmet makes a lot of sense. If you are going high into the mountains and the terrain is going to be rocky then some kind of protective headgear will significantly increase your chances of surviving a headlong plunge down a scree slope, even it is quite possible to get concussion — as did the technical editor of this book — by landing on your face rather than the bit covered by the helmet...

Traditional racing helmets are all but useless for mountain biking, being little more than thin strips of padding with lots of air in between. They are used purely by racing cyclists looking for some semblance of protection in case they fall onto the road.

Climbing, caving or motorcycle helmets are often made from glass fibre and this is rather heavy. They are also too warm to use when cycling as the rider's usual level of exertion means that the body generates quite a lot of heat and a heavy, unventilated

helmet traps this rather effectively at the very place your body is trying to lose it from.

A real cycling helmet will be much lighter and properly ventilated and these two points are essential. It must also be very tough and protect the head efficiently, so most cyclists' helmets will be made from some form of lightweight 'plastic' material such as moulded ABS or polycarbonate. They are very light and you will probably soon forget you are wearing one.

Specifications and model availablity have a habit of changing but names worth looking for include Bell, Kiwi, Nolan, Max and Bike Lid. All are well suited to mountain bike riding but you can consider yourself lucky if your local bike shop has more than two to choose from.

A helmet must fit properly so take your time with your selection. Try on a variety of different models if possible and don't be afraid to walk around the shop for a few minutes with a helmet on to see if you are happy with your choice.

Nolan helmets

Chapter Five

Head for the Hills

ONE of the most refreshing aspects of the growth in mountain bike riding in Britain (for all it is still in its infancy) is the interest it has created among enthusiasts of the outdoors generally. People more accustomed to parading around the hills and mountains on foot are starting to see some of the possibilities the mountain bike offers, with fun and adventure usually being pretty high on the list. For such people, the next few paragraphs may be superfluous but those comparatively new to the glories of upland Britain should read and digest them.

Mountains are dangerous. There are crags to fall over, rocks to trip over and deep bogs waiting for the unwary. Often, the weather can change dramatically in an astonishingly short time and some mountain storms have to be experienced to believed.

Thick cloud can have you pinned against a hillside, torrential rain can soak you even through the best waterproofs and one wrong decision, one wrong choice of route or one mistake in your map-reading can be fatal. This may all sound melodramatic, but it is far from fiction. Ask any mountain rescue team member.

It is all too easy to get yourself into trouble on the uplands. You only have to sprain your ankle in the middle of no-where for a real drama to begin. If you find that you can't go on, then you could be stuck on the mountains for hours until someone finds you, ample time for you to

....deep bogs waiting for the unwary........

start to display the first signseedless to of exposure/ hypothermia. With luck, you might be found before nightfall but if you are out all night then you could quite easily be dead by morning. Really, it's as easy as that.

Clearly, mountains and uplands have to be taken very seriously and while there is no good reason why you should not go there, only a fool would go unpreparedand unready to follow a few basic rules.

Clothing

One of the quickest and most effective ways of getting yourself into serious trouble is to get wet. And as British mountains seem to get rained on with monotonous regularity, it goes without saying that getting wet is usually quite easy. Good waterproofs are therefore not a luxury, they are essential.

Cheap waterproof jackets and over-trousers are usually made from nylon, coated with either polyurethane or silicone. They keep water out but also keep the body's moisture, sweat, in and the result is something like a mobile greenhouse. This is less of a problem for walkers, who by and large generate far less body heat than a cyclist, but for a bike rider they can be a nightmare — you can become completely soaked in condensation in quite a short time.

The best waterproofs use a 'breathing' fabric such as Gore Tex and this keeps the rain out but allows moisture generated by the body to escape through microscopic holes. Needless to say they are expensive — some as £200 or more. There are many other breathable fabrics on the market — Cyclone, Sympatex and Vita-Dry, for example — but so far only Sympatex seems in any way comparable to Gore Tex,

for a long time the market leader. There are few good Gore Tex cycling jackets on the market but most simple, mid-thigh length jackets or cagoules should serve admirably. Two-way zips are a must to enable you to loosen the bottom half of the jacket and give your legs more room for pedalling while the top half is well zipped up against the rain. Overtrousers to match make a lot of sense too as any wet clothing will be uncomfortable and will sap your energy reserves, sometimes alarmingly.

But riding a bike is always liable to produce far more sweat than you can squeeze out fellwalking and many cyclists have been getting disillusioned by Gore Tex and its fellow fabrics because it too is not immune to the 'greenhouse effect'. As a result an old fashioned lightly woven two-layer unwaxed cotton called Ventile has come back into favour. Also worth considering — and at a fraction of the price of Gore Tex — is lightweight oiled cotton or the latest Nikwax TX10-treated fibre pile with Pertex membrane.

The good old fashioned cycling cape is well ventilated from the bottom but it doesn't make a lot of sense on a mountain.It obscures your sight of the ground beneath and behind your front wheel which is the last thing you want when trying to negotiate obstacles. Perhaps even more seriously, it can sometimes act like a spinnaker once the wind hits it. Then again, you will look considerably less of a jerk walking into a restaurant or pub dressed in a Gore Tex or any other kind of jacket than in a great billowing cape...

Cycling shoes are too flexible and the soles too smooth for mountain use, but there is nothing wrong in wearing training shoes for off-road work. But I generally wear light walking boots. I feel safer wearing them as I am less likely to turn an ankle, they make walking across difficult, rocky or loose terrain easier and more comfortable and I don't have to worry about getting my feet wet storming through bogs.

While a boot will be more supportive, some people (with stronger ankles) prefer the extra movement you get in walking shoes.

Mountain bike boots are beginning to make an appearance though as I write it would seem that most manufacturers are simply plugging a gap in the market without really understanding what the mountain biker needs. Some I have looked at are little more than macho baseball boots. Though certainly lighter and (in some cases) more comfortable than lightweight walking boots, they can still become out of their depth on the mountains, especially in the wet. If conditions under foot are fairly dry, then by all means wear them but for really serious mountain biking a decent lightweight boot or walking shoe will stand you in much better stead. The general requirement is a deep patterned sole for good grip, combined with hard insteps and soles.

The rest of your clothing can be fairly standard cycling garb — shorts, jersey or track suit top. A woolly training cap is also a good idea, especially in cold weather. Avoid wearing heavy clothing — it is far better to wear two or three thin layers than one heavy one as this enables you to adjust your body temperature far more easily, adding one layer if you begin to cool, removing one layer if you begin to overheat. Wind chill must also be reckoned upon so make sure your top layer is windproof, a polycotton jacket, for example. And don't forget that your waterproof top is also windproof and therefore warming.

A spare pair of trousers is an eminently good idea. Shorts are fine to cycle in but wind chill can become severe on mountain tops and you will feel this particularly when you stop for food and a rest. A pair of tracksuit trousers, especially those designed specifically for cycling (these fit snugly around the ankles and don't catch on the chainset) are ideal as they can be pulled on in a trice and are comfortable enough to ride in if needs be. Another solution would be to don a pair of waterproof trousers — warming, certainly, but not quite as comfortable next to the skin.

Equipment

You have to be prepared for almost anything if you venture deep into the hills, so you will need to carry more than just sandwiches and a spare inner tube.

Always carry spare clothing. If you are forced to stop you might find yourself cooling down at an alarming rate and this is a surefire way of developing hypothermia. It is therefore essential you retain as much body heat as possible, so put another jersey or a jacket on when you stop, even if you are still sweating. It sounds a little weird, but is standard mountain practice. Be prepared for the temperature to be a lot lower on top than it is in the valley — 0.6C colder for every 100m you climb, or about 3°F per thousand feet. And that's not even allowing for wind chill.

A good Ordnance Survey map is essential and the Landranger Series (1:50,000 scale) is ideal. If you are planning a tough ascent of one or a group of mountains then choose the 1:25,000 series as this has far more detail and was invaluable on my ascent of Ben Nevis. If your map reading is a little rusty then get a book out of the library, study it and above all practise. You should also stop frequently and get used to interpreting your position by using the map — even if you know where you are, check the map at your next logical stopping point and take a close look around you, checking features on the map with how they look in real life. The Dalesman Publishing Company does a very handy little book called, simply, Map Reading which won't break your pocket. It's by Robert B Matkin (ISBN 0 85206 769 0).

A compass is also essential. If you don't know how to use one you've obviously never been a Scout or Guide — ask someone for advice or consult Matkin or another book on the subject. It only takes the cloud to drop a few thousand feet for you to find yourself totally lost and people who are lost can quite easily get themselves into more serious trouble, like becoming exhausted or cycling off a crag.

Go for a fairly simple compass to begin with — there are some excellent models in the Silva range — and use it regularly so that you become confident in using it. It might save your skin one day.

A compass from the Silva range

Always assume that you are going to be out on the hills longer than you intend to be. Make sure you have plenty of food. I normally pack an ample supply of sand-wiches (for 'ample' read 'more than enough') plus a few small high energy items such as bananas, Austrian smoked cheeses, bags of raisins, Trailmix (the sort of 'muesli in a bag') and the like. A bar of chocolate or Kendal mint cake can also be a useful stand-by.

Fluids are less of a problem as you can usually find a burn, beck or stream to quench your thirst (this applies only to Britain, be wary of drinking water in hotter countries as you never know what bugs may be living in it). You will probably want to carry some fluid with you anyway — I normally take milk or fresh orange juice as both are refreshing and have a small (but significant) energy content.

Anything else? Well, a whistle is useful if you get into trouble and a Swiss Army knife also has a host of uses. All the usual tools and spares for your bike should also be carried (see Survivial Servicing chapter), and don't forget to pack at least some semblance of a first aid kit — a selection of plasters, a tube of antiseptic cream, lint and a crepe bandage should be regarded as the absolute minimum. If you can afford one, an altimeter is a useful team-mate for your compass when the cloud comes down and will double as a barometer to warn of impending weather changes. Cheap ones start at about £25.

There are two ways of carrying all this equipment — either on the bike or on the rider.

If I am going to put in some mileage on the road then I usually opt for panniers as these put all the weight low down at the back of the bike, by far then best place to carry weight. Riding a bike with a ruck-sack on your back is not particularly com-fortable because your back tends to sweat quite a lot. However, in an off-road excursion your panniers can make the bike heavy and prone to lunging from side to side. The situation becomes worse the more weight you carry. Similarly, the chances of breaking your paniers on rough ground increases with the load in them. It is also possible for the panniers to foul on rocks and obstructions, and they make the bike heavy to push or carry.

Rucksacks, hipsacks and bumbags enable the bike to be light, manoeuverable and predictable in the way it handles.

For a short day trip in the mountains I normally carry a rucksack, about 35 litres in capacity. This gives ample room for all the equipment I will need so weight will not be much of a problem. But if the rucksack starts to fill up then it is time to consider panniers, especially if some of the route is along roads or well defined tracks. If your chosen route is rougher then opt for a combination of the two and try to spread the weight around a little. This is the system you should adopt if you are planning a two or three-day off-road trip, especially if you are carrying lightweight camping gear. But the golden rule really is to tailor the severity of your route to the amount of luggage you have to take with you.

Preparation

There should always be an element of planning in any trip into the mountains. This involves tracing your proposed route with the aid of a map.

You don't have to plan down to the last detail but it is essential for you to be familiar with the terrain and countryside into which you are riding. You can change direction at any time during the course of a ride but you can only really do this if you

The author on a mountain trip — the load is on the rider, not on the bike

have a good idea of the surrounding countryside and its features. There is no point in changing your course only to find yourself stranded on top of a mountain miles and miles from home. Orientation is the key. Get to know the mountains around you, first on the map and then in the field. Identify key features — lakes, fords, trig points or sharp deviations in the track — and tick them off in your mind as you pass them.

When you are planning a route on the map, always assume that disaster will strike. Weather conditions can change with staggering speed and ferocity in the mountains and you might find yourself having to bail out in a hurry. Using the map, try to identify possible escape routes — tracks or paths which will get you off the mountain top and into the valley safely and quickly. Abortive action like this can be called for even in summer so it is well worth working out an escape plan before you venture out. If nothing else, it will help you to familiarise yourself with the landscape over which you will be riding.

Don't assume that every track and footpath marked on the map will be ideal for off road riding. Many will not be and quite a few tracks will hardly be discernible at all on the ground. Remember that a string of dots or a broken line on a map indicates only a right of way and not a well surfaced mountain highway.

And always go prepared for the worst. It probably won't happen but it's no good being stuck in the middle of nowhere wishing you had brought an extra jersey or more food. Situations like this are potentially dangerous — never have any doubts about that.

Taking a mountain bike into the mountains is the most exciting and the highest form of ATB riding. It can be extremely challenging, immensely satisfying, the views can be tremendous and the riding can really get the adrenalin flowing. But mountains must also be taken very seriously, especially remote mountain areas.

Don't forget that.

Dressed for the part — the author on Ben Nevis

Chapter Seven

Where to Ride

IN July 1984, the American outdoor magazine Backpacker carried the following news story:

According to Doug Scott, Director of Federal Affairs of the Sierra Club, the question of off-road bikes in Federal wilderness is open and shut. Citing the 1964 Wilderness Act, Scott stated that the club's position is that those 'other forms of mechanical travel' which are expressly forbidden on wilderness lands by the Act, clearly include bicycles.

In fact, the Sierra Club was apparently approached by the National Off-Road Bicycle Association for support in gaining access for bicycles to wilderness trails... according to Scott, they found some documentation provided by some California-based members that the danger of trail damage was apparently quite real. Members reported deep ruts and soil erosion caused by tyre tracks, especially where the bikes braked coming down hills.

In Britain that same month, the environmental pressure group Friends of the Earth published a consultation paper called Environmental and Other Implications of the Growth in Off-Highway Cycling, which included the following observations:

There may be a perceived 'clash' of interests between various groups which demand access to recreational facilities in the countryside. It may be felt that the increased usage of the bicycle in areas which have not previously been accessible to the cyclist will lead to an erosion of 'rights', or perhaps even serious damage to the environment.

Taking both of these excerpts together, there are three points to consider. Firstly, rights of access and the law which governs whether you should be there or not, secondly the possibility of damage to the countryside from overabundant or over-enthusiastic ATB use and finally the potential clash of interests between mountain bikers and other outdoor enthusiasts — walkers, climbers, birdwatchers and the like.

It is essential that you understand what each of these points is about before you even venture off-road with your mountain bike.

The Law

Unfortunately, while the law regarding the use of bicycles off-road appears fairly clear cut, its interpretation is somewhat less so. Indeed, having spoken to various police authorities throughout Britain, I have found inconsistencies in the way the laws are interpreted.

Basically, the situation in England and Wales is as follows. Bicycles are allowed to use ordinary metalled roads. You are also allowed to ride your bike on

45

bridleways, unless there is a specific local bye law prohibiting you, but you must give way to horseriders and walkers at all times. That is clear cut.

Cyclists are not allowed to use footpaths where they run parallel to roads (pavements, for example). This would seem to suggest that paths across open moorland, miles from the nearest road, are fine for riding along — but this is not necessarily so. The problem here surrounds the use of a bicycle on a public right of way but across private land.

Technically, wherever there is a public right of way, you have a right to be there but it is possible that private landowners whose land is crossed by a right of way will object to your being there with your bike. Quite what the outcome of legal proceedings in a case like this would be is difficult to predict. If it could be proved that you had trespassed to obtain access to a public right of way, or had trespassed while riding along a public right of way, the case might be found against you. Similarly, you might be sued for any damage you caused.

To my knowledge, there have been no test cases in this respect so a precedent has yet to be set.

Private roads or tracks (which are not recognised rights of way) are out of bounds to the cyclist. This includes Forestry Commission tracks, unless specific permission has been granted, and tracks owned by quarry and mining companies. Green roads, tracks across open countryside, are fine as long as they are recognised rights of way.

You can check on these at your county or regional council headquarters, which will have a Roads and Highways Department and possibly also a Rights of Way Officer.

But always remember that a footpath marked on a map does not always imply a right of way. If in doubt, check it out.

Open spaces under the control of local authorites (parks, for example) are usually off-limits to cyclists under local byelaws. Only in a very few cases, like Hyde Park, London, are you allowed to ride through a park and then only along selected routes.

Disused railway lines seem to offer the off-road cyclist ideal opportunities for interesting cross-country travel but here too there can be problems. The British Railways Board has a policy of selling off sections of disused trackbed to the owners of land over which the railway once passed. As a result, virtually all disused railway line is in private hands, so permission to use it must be sought.

Canal towpaths are also out of bounds, though you can obtain a permit from the British Waterways Board to use towpaths in a particular region. There is a small fee but the BWB has often shown great reluctance in awarding these permits.

Now that we have all become thoroughly depressed, perhaps I ought to rephrase all of this in more positive terms — wherever there is a public right of way, you can ride your bike (just as long as that public right of way does not run alongside a road).

There, that sounds a little more promising, doesn't it? Just remember that, while you are committing no criminal offence, nor do you have any specific **right** to ride on a public footpath. Additionally, some areas of open country, like moorland, fell and coastal areas, are open to public use by established custom or consent, and that consent sometimes includes riding bicycles. A useful booklet called Out in the Country is available from the Countryside Commission's Publications Department, 19/23 Albert Road, Manchester M19 2EQ.

In Scotland the law is rather different — the right of cyclists to use foot rights of way appears clear. But unlike England and Wales where there is a Definitive Map of rights of way (again held by your local highways department), it is not so easy to establish where such rights exist north of the border.

The subject is dealt with further in the next chapter.

First, Find your Route

Your first view of a possible route will probably be from the comfort of your armchair — with the aid of a map. First, let's decide what a cross-country route looks like on paper.

The routes we are looking for can be divided into three general categories — tracks, bridleways and footpaths. The word 'track' is used in its loosest sense and can mean either a rough, gravelly road (something like a Forestry Commission road), a rough rocky track leading to a farm say, a 'green road' of much greater antiquity than either of the first two, or indeed a disused railway track. The point is that it is a broad way, certainly broad enough to accommodate some form of motorised four-wheeled transport and possibly still used by four-wheel drive vehicles or tractors.

Tracks can be recognised on an Ordnance Survey map by a pair of parallel broken lines between which there is no colouring. Solid black lines denote some form of fencing or hedge and are usually (though not always) 'made-up' or tarmac-ed. These are less fun than the true cross-country rough track.

Such tracks are perfect for gaining access to more remote areas of the uplands. Most will be traffic-free, fairly evenly surfaced and will enable you to cover ground quite quickly. However, few can be described as being particularly challenging so you may not want to spend the whole day running along a pair of wheel tracks — with one or two exceptions, cross-country tracks of 30 or 40 mile are pretty thin on the ground.

Bridleways are marked by a single broken red line on the 1:50,000 OS map and a dashed green line on the 1:25,000 series. If there can sometimes be a little doubt concerning the ownership of tracks and whether or not you have a right to be there, there is — subject to the provisos already mentioned — no such doubt regarding bridleways.

Bridleways can be something of a lottery. Often they are broad, smooth and firm of surface. Equally often, they can be carved to ribbons by a hundred horses' hooves — rough going in dry weather and very, very muddy in wet. Still, where rough tracks fear to tread, the bridleway will often go on, plunging ever deeper into the country-side or the mountains. Some can be pretty challenging, too. Don't expect to cover as many miles on a bridleway as on a green road or track — most will force you to take more time but with the bonus that this usually adds to the enjoyment.

Footpaths are marked as single dotted thin red lines on the 1:50,000 map (much thinner than those marking a bridleway) and as green dotted lines on the 1:25,000 series. These are often the most challeng-ing of the three types of route I am describing. To begin with, a line of dashes on a map does not imply a well surfaced cross-country route. Some can be barely visible, others completely buried beneath the countryside. Some can even be buried under crops, thanks to unscrupulous farmers. In short, footpaths **can** be quite obscure. In lowland areas, your progress

47

will often be interrupted by a stile or gate every hundred yards or so, though moorland, heathland or mountain routes will usually be free from such obstructions. They can still be pretty tough, however — steep, rough, rocky, sinuous. In short, great fun! It is difficult to know what a path looks like just from the map, however, so perhaps these are even more of a lottery than the bridleway but that can be little excuse for not getting out there and finding out. Do that often enough and you will find some absolutely gorgeous paths tracing their way across the countryside and often these are the one's that look the least promising. Remember, though, the legal status of footpaths and the fact that you have no specific right to ride on them. Use common sense, or seek permission from the landowner.

Where to Ride — Legally!

Only you will be able to decide on the type of mountain biking you want to do. One of the great problems (and, conversely, one of the great joys) of mountain biking is that the machine itself simply encourages you to go further, higher, harder — the only limit is your personal sense of adventure.

Often, the more obvious routes are a little disappointing. For the real off-road enthusiast a long distance footpath such as the Peninne Way might seem ideal for a long, challenging tour. In fact, most of this 260-mile route is very heavy going and not at all suited to mountain biking. Furthermore it is a **footpath** and, because of the legal anomalies already described there are strong arguments for mountain bikers to steer clear of such a prominent pedestrian route.

Likewise, routes through lower country-side can become something of a pain. If your route takes you through arable land or pasture then you will probably have a million stiles to cross or gates to negotiate.

Bridleways offer more scope but there are few continuous stretches longer than five or six miles and it is often only when you can successfully combine three or four sections with a couple of stretches of footpath that you can realistically say that you have had a good day out on the mountain bike.

The problems I have just outlined are more often associated with lowland routes, though there are obvious exceptions. For example, there are sizeable swathes of heathland in Surrey and Hampshire (and many other counties) which are fairly low lying but offer great possibilities to the off-road cyclist. Consult local bye-laws first, though. Other lowland routes include the Peddars Way (see next chapter) in Norfolk, which consists of byways, bridle-way and disused railway line, and there are many more low-level, cross-country routes of considerable distance throughout Britain.

Upland routes often offer greater scope. Population is usually more sparse and agriculture less intensive so routes can run for miles and miles without interruption. Frequently, upland routes are the remains of ancient trade routes which criss-crossed the country and considerable stretches of these ancient 'motorways' remain today. The Ridgeway, running from the depths of Wiltshire almost to the fringes of London, is an obvious example and there are many others besides.

Usually, the higher you ride the tougher it gets, so routes through some of Britain's more mountainous areas can be extremely challenging. If it is real mountains you want then you will probably find yourself being pushed to the limit in terms of strength, stamina and riding technique. Summit bagging in areas like the Lake District, North Wales or the Highlands of Scotland is no picnic and your routes will often look a lot easier on the map than they do on the ground. But going for big mountains can be extremely rewarding. I felt great after climbing Ben Nevis in May 1986 — cold, wet and tired, too — though I doubt if I would do it again with quite as much blind enthusiasm.

Highland routes are often very wet and the terrain difficult. Footpaths marked in bold on your map can often be barely discernible scrapes in the wet ground. But don't let any of this put you off because riding a mountain bike in the highlands of Britain is about as close to nirvana as any of us mortals has a right to expect. If, like me, you enjoy pushing yourself and your bike to the limit then this is the kind of terrain you will adore.

Trips like this need no small degree of planning and a great deal of awareness (see chapter five).

But routes through the mountains need not always be epic affairs. Study your map carefully and you will find a host of comparatively easy routes through spectacular scenery. The West Highland Way even as far up as Glencoe is a case in point, Mastiles Lane in the Yorkshire Dales another, and there are many more. But bear in mind that some of these easier routes will be less obvious — some that look easy on the map can be very difficult on the ground and the reverse can also be true.

So some will only be discovered when you actually come to ride them. Always go prepared for a few surprises.

The ATB Rider's Code

If you go for some of the more obvious routes, such as the South Downs Way, the West Highland Way or tracks in the more popular mountain areas, then you will

You know, sometimes I get a sort of gut feeling ...

....go prepared for a few surprises....

almost certainly come across other outdoor enthusiasts. This might lead to a certain hostility — but only if you let it. There is absolutely no reason why ramblers, mountaineers, hill-walkers and nature lovers should not co-exist quite happily with the mountain bike rider and you have a responsibilty to ensure that this happens.

If there is not already a Code of Conduct for mountain bike riders in the British countryside then I beg no forgiveness for formulating one here and now. Knives have already been drawn in certain circles and it is up to us all to ensure that they are never used in anger against us.

It is very easy to intimidate other people if you are riding a bike along a footpath or bridleway — don't! If the path is narrow, slow down or dismount and give them right of way. This should usually be accompanied by a friendly 'Good Morning, nice day, isn't it?' or similar. This melts the hearts of even the most hostile of ramblers and will usually lead to a bout of friendly conversation something along the lines of 'Gosh, you must be mad/keen/very fit to bring a bike up here! How much did it cost you? How many gears — 15?!!'

They will leave with a favourable impression of mountain bike riders in general and when they meet another further along the path will probably be more interested than annoyed. .

Don't come up behind walkers unannoun- ced. Say 'hello' at a discreet distance and slow down. There is nothing more annoying than some fool on a mountain bike hurtling past your ear having appeared out of nowhere. Most walkers will stop, turn round and perhaps even step off the path. This is a courtesy you must always return. The most obvious time to

do so is when you are approaching a group of walkers heading towards you.

Observe the Country Code at all times. The parts of this which are relevant to mountain bikers call for:

- A general respect of the life and work of the countryside
- Guarding against fire
- Keeping gates fastened (except where obviously kept open by a farmer with good reason)
- Sticking to the public right of way across farmland and using gates and stiles to cross fences, hedges and walls
- Not interfering with livestock or machinery
- Litter to be taken home, wildlife plants and trees protected and unnecessary noise avoided.

Some people equate mountain bikes with motorbikes and imagine that the tyres on your bike will cause just as much damage to paths and trails as a 350cc trials machine. Bear this in mind. Erosion is a major problem in popular tourist areas and while rear wheel slides might look impressive they also carve up the countryside and brand you as a wally. Behave responsibly at all times.

Mountain bikes can easily become a problem if we all behave stupidly. But if we show that we can be just as responsible as the next man (or woman) then we will all be treated with respect rather than hostility. Behave like an idiot and the guy further back down the trail might come in for a rough time.

And that guy might be you. Or me.

Rubbing Salt in the Wound

And now, a cautionary tale about what can happen when you try and put some of this chapter's lessons into practice. It's all too easy to form romantic notions about off-road routes and Salters' Road, one of my own favourites, is a case in point. It was not simply the name that first appealed to me but the fact that it was attached to an obscure bridleway crossing one of the more remote areas of the Cheviots, the high but lonely hills which divide England from Scotland.

I first discovered this route by chance. Someone had mentioned Salters' Road while talking about a walk they had done in the Cheviots. The name stuck in my mind and my curiosity was aroused when I spotted it on a map I was poring over. I traced its route and to my surprise noticed that it stretched for some considerable distance, starting on low ground to the east and heading north-west, finally to cross the border into Scotland. A suitable off-road route, I wondered...

But that name puzzled me. Why should a remote bridleway be so called? I mentioned the name to a friend who was interested in local history who told me that salt had been produced on the coast of Northumberland in the 17th and 18th centuries. A visit to the local history section of my library confirmed this and furnished more clues to the Salters' Way. Mine owners panned sea water for salt and exported the produce all over the country. Seventeenth century Britain was scarcely well endowed with roads so the loads went by pack horse to all points of the compass.

Pack horses bound for Scotland faced either a long detour or a rugged journey over the Cheviots. It seemed likely that many of them opted for the shorter, tougher route and so the path they carved over the hills become known as the Salters' road.

This, of course, was all conjecture; I had still to find hard documentary evidence to support my theory. But with the image of this perhaps forgotten trade route firmly implanted in my mind, I determined to find out what was left of it.

I studied the map carefully and found an access road where I could get the car to a point close to the start of the route. Park by the church, a mile or two of footpath and I would be on Salters' Road. Great.

This is where things started to go wrong. After the hour's drive to the Cheviots, I looked for the footpath, marked clearly on the map as running alongside the churchyard. There was no sign of it. The route would have taken me through a meadow so deep it was all but impenetrable. I opted to ride a few miles along a farm road and pick up my route further on.

I was having doubts about the trip. It might have been several hundred years since Salters' Road saw any appreciable traffic and it could be all but impossible to find any evidence of it on the ground. As it turned out, I was both right and wrong.

The map suggested that Salters' Road disappeared under a short section of unfenced but tarmac-ed road and it was to this point that I was riding. Imagine my surprise — and delight — when I discovered that Salters' Road had not disappeared under the heather but was clearly printed into the hillside.

My first sight of the route was an uncharacteristically straight section of tarmac heading straight as an arrow towards the hills and Scotland. There was a farm built across its path now but, off-road at last, I tackled the steep climb with innocent enthusiasm.

The going was certainly rough but the track was clearly defined. Once on the top, I was going to really start enjoying this. However, once the rutted track had levelled out I was faced with a problem. Salters' Road suddenly disappeared into a million other broad tracks, none of which seemed to be heading in the right direction. Clearly, the section I had just cycled along was still in occasional use by farmers and sheep but both had forged new tracks from the summit at a later date.

In a case like this, map and compass are essential, though on this occasion even they were of limited use. Following the course of Salters' Road as closely as I could, I discovered that the route promptly disappeared into a wide expanse of deep heather. Riding was impossible and tracing the route not much easier.

Once you lose sight of your track, but plough on regardless in roughly the right direction, you are tempted to accept any re-emerging track as the right one. On the other side of the heather field I found such a track and was convinced it was the right one. I was wrong and went a long way off the route, although I managed to make a pretty good day of it, despite making such a stupid and elementary mistake.

I returned to Salters Road on several more occasions, tracing its tortuous route through the Cheviots as far as the Scottish border. Some sections are clearly marked on the ground, others are indistinct to say the least. Intersecting sheep tracks readily confuse the eye and the work of the Forestry Commission doesn't always help matters. Though clearly marked on the map, the track is often very ambiguous on the ground.

The moral of the story is that routes which look exciting/ideal/challenging on an Ordnance Survey sheet don't always turn out the way you want them to. You might find yourself having to spend more time staring at the map than at the scenery and this can become a bore. Still, the only way to find out if the route is a good one is to get out there, ride it and make your own discoveries.

While that is what mountain biking is all about for many people, there are times when you might be more than happy to have somebody else do the research work for you, and the following chapter offers a selection of tried and tested routes with that in mind.

If they whet your appetite, perhaps you too will want to try your hand at tracing some of Britain's ancient trade routes...(see Bibliography for suggested references).

Chapter Eight

Go forth and Cycle

THE suggested routes in this chapter are aimed at offering a variety of rides in different scenery — they are **not** intended to provide a comprehensive atlas of off-road routes in Britain. With the problems of footpath riding explained in the previous chapter very much in mind, the selected routes stick to tracks where the rider need expect no dispute as to his or her right to be there.

The routes are all in England and Wales — the knowledge that you can quite legitimately cycle on a foot right of way in Scotland is tempered by the difficulty in establishing that a particular route is a right of way.

We can do no better than quote the advice of Arthur Phillipps at the Glentress Mountain Bike Centre, Peebles, that you negotiate directly with the estate factor. If you want the legwork done for you, contact Arthur at the address in the directory section — his centre supplies, for a modest fee, maps and instructions for following routes in the Borders which he has negotiated.

Meanwhile, if riders establish good routes of their own — in Scotland or elsewhere — Leading Edge will be pleased to receive them to help compile a comprehensive directory.

Quantock Hills, Somerset

Start: *Holford Village*
Distance: *27km/16.8 miles, none on road*
Terrain: *Wooded combes rising to bracken and heather hill tops.*
Going: *Rough stony paths and stream crossings.*
Maps: *OS Landranger (1:50,000) sheet 181 (182); OS Pathfinder (1:25,000) sheets ST04/14 and ST03/13.*

YOU really need a car or stamina for this one, because you'll have to do an extra 27.3 km (17 miles) if you take the train to Taunton and ride up from there. It's about the same from Bridgewater station, but, being a smaller station, fewer trains stop

there...You could make a weekend of it, though, couldn't you?

Park your bike transporter in the large lay-by just above Holford village. Approaching by the A39 from Bridgewater to Minehead, it's to your left on a wide, sweeping right hand bend, about half a mile before Holford.

There's a small tarmac lane off the lay-by which leads to Holford Combe. Take this for about ten yards and turn left onto a bridleway signed 'To Crowcombe'.

Ride up this hill until it meets some deciduous woods on your right. Look out for a narrow path into these woods. Take it until you emerge, after a gentle descent, onto a more clearly defined track into Holford Combe.

53

Follow the course of the stream along Holford Combe, which involves crossing it several times, until you reach the parting of the combes; into Lady's Combe and Frog Combe. Now, don't take either of these, but head, more or less straight on, slightly to your right, up a very loose steep stony track.

After getting up there somehow, this track levels out and becomes grassy.

Continue ahead, going straight over the crossing with another track and skirt Wilmot's Pool to your left before a short descent towards a tarmac lane. Avoid the road by forking right to Crowcombe Park Gate, and left to Crowcombe Combe Gate. Cross the lane and follow the track along the ridge to Triscombe Stone, where there is a car park.

Pass Triscombe Stone and the track now borders a coniferous plantation. When it begins to rise and becomes stony, fork right, pass a junction, and fork right again at the next. This will bring you to 'Pit (disused)'. Here you can prove the map wrong by using said pit for all kinds of unmentionable antics, but not lunch...yet.

All good things must come to an end; so mount your steed and head off up the path which runs alongside the pit. This takes you to the highest point in the Quantocks — Wills Neck. And the view to be had from here makes this the stop for eats.

Continue ahead until the path begins its descent in earnest, when a right turn will bring you back down to Triscombe Stone. Look out for your tyre tracks and retrace your previous route as far as Crowcombe Park Gate, then continue on this broad track along the ridge, keeping to the newly erected fence, up over Hurley Beacon, past Halsway Soggs, past Halsway Post and on to Bicknoller Post, being sure to veer right at Lowsey Thorn.

By continuing in this direction you'll cross 'The Great Road', which is, in fact, a trackway, and, cresting Beacon Hill, look for a grassy track to your right. Take this, and after a short distance, descend to the left of a small coniferous platation.

This delightful descent is considered one of the best in the Quantocks. It is quite steep and stony until you ford the stream and enter Smith's Combe, which you should follow right to the bottom, savouring every moment, diving in out of the stream as you go.

When Smith's Combe begins to open out into the valley, and crosses the stream for the last time, turn right and climb round the ridge. Keeping pasture to your left and rough to your right, down into, and up out of, Dens Combe, fork right soon after. Head due south until you reach New Ground, go straight across, bearing left and taking the track that skirts Longstone Hill, on down into Hodder's Combe and through the river.

At this point you can take a short-cut home by turning left and lopping some 5km, or about three miles, off the route.

But we know you'll be wanting more. So, turn right and go up the combe until you reach the next ford. Here take the left fork up an ill-defined path along Somerton Combe. Up the headland where Stert Combe joins Somerton Combe, ascend, first climbing at an angle veering to the right, then making a zigzag left along the contour and right, up along the ridge.

At the top you'll come to a T-junction at which you should turn left, following this track, past two paths to the left, until you reach a cross-tracks, with the left arm running along the spine of Black Hill. Take this, passing Higher Hare Knap to your left. Continue downhill until the grassy track levels out slightly and you come to

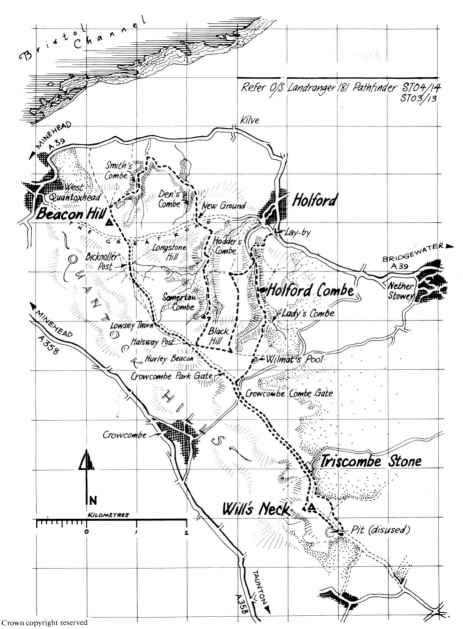

Refer O/S Landranger 181 Pathfinder ST04/14 ST03/13

the next cross-tracks, turn right.

This descent will bring you down with a splash into Holford Combe again. But a little cautionary note here ... there is a BOG, a small one perhaps, but a real live genuine lesser spotted Bog. (For the cheats I will tell you that it can be avoided by skirting around to the left.)

At this point you have four options:

1) turn right for a second lap, 2) turn left for Holford Village and welcome refreshment, 3) retrace your tyre tracks up the other side of the combe to return to the car park.

The South Downs Way

Start: *Buriton (map ref 740 200)*
Finish: *Eastbourne (map ref 598 983)*
Distance: *80 miles, bridleway*
Maps: *OS 1:50,000 sheets 197,198, 199*
Publications: *South Downs Way by Sean Jennett, HMSO. The South Downs Way, published by the Youth Hostels Association.*

OPENED in 1972, this was the first long distance path with bridleway status over its whole length. It follows the ridge of the chalk downland in what Kipling called 'those great whale backs'. Apart from some steep gradients crossing the river valleys, the going is good. Much of the route is chalk and flint, which can be slippery in the wet. Don't forget it is a bridleway; the mud can be daunting in places on the eastern sections, especially around Jevington. The majority of the route is over 600ft, the highest point being 837ft and is quite exposed, on the downs themselves there is little shelter once away from the trees. There are roads and bridleways leading to villages and hamlets, crossing and joining the Way all along its length, so food and shelter are never far away.

The Weald and Downland Open Air Museum at Singleton, two miles south of the way at Cocking, and the Chalk Pits Museum at Amberley are well worth visiting. The whole of the Way is littered with prehistoric tumuli, Stone Age, Iron Age and Roman remains. A wonderful ride, especially in the summer, but can be demanding in wet weather.

It is possible to ride mostly on bridleways to the New Forest 63 miles to the west, and by the Downs Link, to the North Downs Way 30 miles to the north.

The track from Buriton wends uphill to Harting Downs and then on grassy slopes to Beacon Hill and Philliswood Down. Then by track bordered in parts by woodland, giving way to wonderful views across Hampshire, south of Lynch Down to Cocking Down. This is probably the most isolated and enjoyable stretch of the South Downs Way.

Crossing the A286, the flinty track rises to enter forests along the top of Graffam Downs. Enclosed by woodland, there is little to see, climbing up to Littleton Down, the highest of the Downs. The track descends to cross the A285, rises again, twisting and turning to the summit of Bignor Hill, and crosses the old Roman road of Stane Street. A narrow grassy track descends to cross the A289 and after a mile crosses the River Arun. After a short bit of road, you turn down a quiet country lane past the Amberley Chalk Pits Museum. A steep slippery slope leads you up to Amberley Mount. The character of the Way has changed to open downland

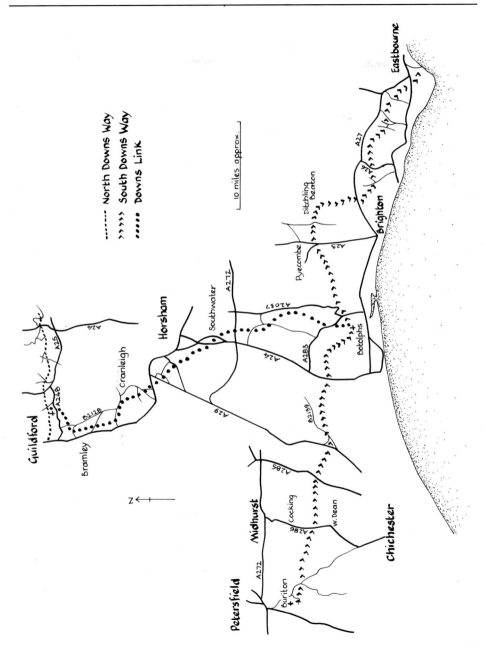

with wonderful views over rounded hills and dry valleys to the sea, and northwards over The Weald to the North Downs.

The track leads you to the summit of Highden Hill. The Way proper is a very badly eroded chalk track, but there is a detour, crossing the A24 via a special riders' and walkers' bridge, to rejoin the South Downs Way south of Washington. Up a chalk track to the top of the downs, and grassy stretches lead you just south of Chanctonbury Ring and over Steyning Round Hill. A hard track leads to a lovely country lane, past Annington Manor and on by road to St. Botolph's Church, where the Downs Link joins the Way. Cross the River Adur on the new bridge, zigzag across the A283, and rise again by road past the Youth Hostel to enjoy another lovely stretch, over Perching Hill and down to Devil's Dyke where there is a self-service cafe. Beware of low flying hang gliders!

The Way crosses the road at the lovely old village of Saddlecombe, then climbs to Pyecombe, crosses the A23, then up past Clayton windmills, popularly known as Jack and Jill. A gentle track meanders along the top of the downs past Ditchling Beacon, well known to London to Brighton riders and on to Plumpton Plain, then turns south over some lovely tracks before descending to cross the A27. The route climbes over Newmarket Hill and Iford Hill, before dropping via Mill Lane into Rodmell. Turn right along the road through Southease and cross the River Ouse, the railway, and the A26. The route twists uphill and meanders to Firle Beacon, another high point with superb all-round views. Watch out for hang gliders again.

Grassy tracks then take you through the market square of Alfriston, and over the River Cuckmere. The Way rises over Windover Hill to Jevington. A deep, sometimes muddy lane takes you to a junction of tracks at the top of the Downs; follow the plinths which mark the bridleway. A slippery track will bring you down into Eastbourne.

The Downs Link

Start: *St Martha's church (map ref: 032 483)*
Finish: *St Botolph's church (map ref: 193 094)*
Distance: *30 miles (bridleway)*
Maps: *OS 1:50,000, sheets,186,187,198*
Publications: *Downs Link, published by Surrey and W.Sussex County Councils and Waverly District Council (available from W. Sussex County Council, County Hall, Chichester, West Sussex, PO19 1RL.*

THIS is an easy going north south route, linking the North and South Downs Ways. The surface is generally good, but there are some muddy sections if you ride in winter or early spring. It is well protected from wind for the most part, a nice quiet ride at any time of the year, particularly beautiful in spring and offering an unusual view of the countryside.

The Link leaves the North Downs Way just east of the 11th century church of St Martha and follows bridleways waymarked down to the Tillingbourne Valley and over sandy wooded heaths and farmland to the village of Bramley. Here it meets the former Horsham and Guildford railway. This then takes you along the old trackbed, which parallels the disused Wey and Arun canal, through a wildlife corridor that offers tantalising glimpses over common and farmland. It is quite heavily wooded in places and rich in natural history.

The Link leaves the original track near Christ's Hospital and after a short country road joins the trackbed of the former Shoreham to Itchingfield Junction railway. You pass through some lovely country over the river Adur then a brief detour through Henfield to join the track again. You are now into Weald country with glorious views over farmland to the South Downs ahead and to the west with Chanctonbury Ring on the ridge. After crossing the Adur south of Stretham

Manor, you detour over the fields and half a mile of road to the roundabout at Bramber.

Bramber Castle is a Norman fortress built in 1083 on a huge natural mound by the side of the original course of the River Adur. It was the home of the de Braose family, but is now owned by the National Trust. The castle was destroyed during the Civil War, all that is left is a 76ft high section of the keep and the earthworks, but it is still worth visiting

From the roundabout, follow a short section of bypass then join the track for the final stretch to the South Downs Way just north of the church of St Botolph's.

The North Downs Way and Pilgrims' Way (part)

Start: *Guildford*
Finish: *Box Hill*
Distance: *12 miles (bridleway)*
Maps: *OS 1:50,000, sheets 187, 186*
Publication: *The North Downs Way by D Herbstein (HMSO).*

THE North Downs Way, opened in 1978, is intended for walkers, though there are lengthy sections of bridleway in the total of 141 miles. The part described here passes over sand and then chalk as the Way follows the southern edge of the chalk downs escarpment. The surface is variable, the sand being difficult to ride in dry weather, and on the downs there are areas where the chalk is overlaid with clay which, if wet, can only be ridden with difficulty; these sections are generally short. Otherwise the route is easy, but with some steepish hills.

This is a beautiful part of Surrey with some fine chalk downland and thick

deciduous woods on the ridges. There are some stunning views over woods and farmland to the secondary greensand ridge with glimpses of the South Downs in the far distance. The whole area is criss-crossed with bridleways, with many old quarries, offering very varied riding. It is possible to ride a circuit of about 35 miles by going south over the sandy heaths then along the greensand ridge by bridleways over Winterfold, Reynards Hill, Pitch Hill, Holmbury and Leith Hills and then north to Box Hill. With careful map work one can travel further east by linking sections of the North Downs Way by road, and south by the Downs Link to the South Downs.

From Guildford the North Downs Way is waymarked through the northern edge of the Chantries Wood and up the steep track to St Martha's on the Hill with lovely views over Surrey's wooded countryside. The bridleway passes to the south of the church and down to the car park, passing the start of the Downs Link on the way. The North Downs Way from here is a footpath, the best route being via the Pilgrims' Way across the fields, and then a stiff climb up chalky Water Lane to rejoin the Way at Newlands Corner. The Barn cafe here is a popular rendezvous for all cyclists. The route now is the old drove road through woods, past Hollister Farm on to a disused military road. The North Downs Way turns south at the end of the road and becomes a footpath again. Keep on the track ahead which can be very muddy in wet weather. The track joins and runs alongside the road at Ranmore Common then follows the left fork and runs down

through Ashcomb Wood and across fields to the A24 where a subway takes you under the road.

Box Hill is now before you, heavily wooded not only with box but also yew, juniper and whitebeam. To avoid it, going further east, cross the River Mole and follow the bridleways past the quarries to the Buckland Hills and on to Reigate. To get to the top, go north alongside the road past the Burford Bridge Hotel to the road on the right, where you can pick up the bridleway to the top of what is arguably the best known viewpoint in Surrey.

North Downs (2)

Start: *Westcott village; alternatively, Gomshall or Dorking Town stations on the Reading to Redhill line, or Dorking station from Waterloo, Victoria, Holborn or London Bridge; Holmbury St Mary Youth Hostel.*
Distance: *12 miles / 19km, of which 2.5 miles (4km) are on road and the remainder over the rough, across undulating sandstone and chalk, wooded hills. Can be very muddy going, especially in winter.*
Maps: *OS 1:50,000, sheet 187; 1:25,000, sheet.*

BEING situated in the South East, this ride will appear deceptively easy to those for whom elevation is all in terms of achievement in cross-country cycling.
But in the summer or frosty months it makes a most pleasant day jaunt for those who aren't mud fanciers. Although you are never far from civilisation it is wise to carry some survival kit, especially in the winter.

Find yourself on Westcott village green, by whatever means you may, head

towards the Cricketer's pub and take the lane that runs uphill off the main A25. Pass the church on your right and take the next lane on your right. Follow this until the lane veers sharp right, but at this point dive into the woods straight ahead for a little sandy (and cautious) yomping down to the A25 again.

That was simply a better way of getting half a mile down the main road....Now turn sharp left into the drive/track to Rookery Hall Farm. Follow this until it becomes a normal type bridleway contouring up the side of a small valley. Straight ahead you'll see a footpath leading up to the right, but ignore this and veer to the left, following the path until it enters the woods. At this point you have the first, and probably the biggest, challenging hill of the day, so get your trials hat on and plug on up that hill.

At the top turn left to join a broad track that runs the ridge. Stay more or less on the edge of the wood picking the most suitable path to avoid the worst of the mud. Follow this track for nearly a mile and when you reach the crossroads entirely

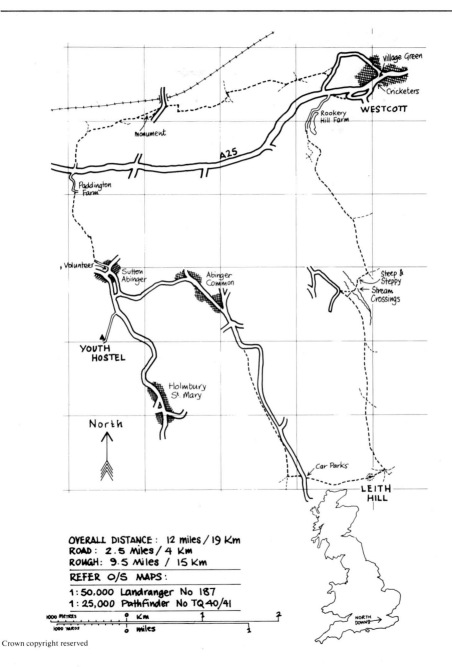

OVERALL DISTANCE: 12 miles / 19 Km
ROAD: 2.5 Miles / 4 Km
ROUGH: 9.5 Miles / 15 Km

REFER O/S MAPS:

1:50,000 Landranger No 187
1:25,000 Pathfinder No TQ 40/41

61

surrounded by woodland, with a Forestry Commission sign up ahead announcing 'Bury Hill' take the track to the right which after a very short distance bears slightly to the right. Continue straight ahead and again bear to the right as the track starts to descend.

The downhill that follows is a right little trials section and fair game, especially if it's been raining. At the bottom of this section join the tarmac drive and continue till you hit road; double back to the left and enjoy this pootling stuff for the next mile or so because it's a long gradual climb on a well used, hard surfaced track.

On reaching the head of this track you'll find a woodland 'Seven Dials'; take the right uphill, and see if you can get all the way up to the top of Leith Hill, where there is a tower, wonderful views, weather permitting, and perhaps the **refreshment booth** will be open.

After your well earned glug of tea and chomp of cake take the track directly opposite your approach and bash on down, taking the left fork till you come to the car parks and the road, though be careful on this last bit because it can be popular with the leg merchants.

Using the Green Cross Code, cross the road and follow the bridleway more or less straight ahead and in the clearing at the bottom turn right onto the well used track. Continue until the road is close by on your right; this bridleway now runs parallel to the road, past High Ashes Farm, and straight ahead.

As the road starts to veer away you'll pass the entrance to 'Dorlin' and a high hedge on your left. Again dive into the woods, when the path turns into one of those classic gullies so often found in this part of the world, which, as usual, will be deep mud along the bottom. However, for the quick witted there's a ledge up on the left bank which will demand a little careful balance, but is usually fairly dry. After this little exercise you soon reach road again by Park House Farm and follow it for a while.

Ignore the first set of junctions, but take the left fork after about half a mile where there is a well in the middle of the fork. At the next junction, after about three quarters of a mile, turn left again and continue past the turning on your left where folks starting their ride at Holmbury St Mary Youth Hostel will be joining the route.

Ride on down to Sutton Abinger where you should turn right, in front of the Volunteer and just beyond the pub turn left up a steep tarmac drive. This drive soon decays into a rough track with grass growing along the centre. At the end don't go through the gate, but turn right and out into the field at the end.

Following the right hand edge of this field, bear left where a footpath crosses and in another 50 yards or so the path runs between two fences, down towards Paddington Farm. Once reached, turn left into the yard and almost immediately right, following the concrete road between the farm buildings. As you leave the farm, the road swings to the left, then to the right, around a silted up mill pond with the old mill on your left and watercress beds beyond the trees.

A little way ahead is the A25 where you would join if starting at Gomshall Station. It's a busy road, so beware. Take the gully opposite where some people chuck their trash to signal their appreciation of its rural charm. Continue to the gate, head across the pasture and into the woods opposite.

In the woods the path bears to the right

and goes through another gate; this is Broomy Downs and Abinger Roughs. Wonderful woodlands, and so popular that they are a maze of well-trod paths. Stick to the main one until it follows the edge of the wood, with fields on your left, and you may catch sight of a train or two — they're getting there. Somewhat further on is a group of farm buildings on your left with a commemorative cross by the path on the right. The inscription is brief and interesting.

Continue, crossing the lane and taking the path at the edge of the woods with a barbed wire fence on the left. After a short distance this path takes a sharp right and a sharp left to follow the edge of the field until you reach the farm which has been visible ahead.

Go down between the barns and turn right along the track between two fields and opposite the front of the farmhouse just passed. There are a few junctions ahead, but simply continue in roughly the same direction and keeping to the main track, which eventually turns into a tarmac lane. Finally this lane takes a turn to the right and you come down to a T-junction where you should turn left to follow the lane back to the village green.

Chiltern Hills

Start: *Wendover railway station*
Distance: *11 miles/ 17.7km, of which 3.5 miles (5.6km) are on road, the remainder on the rough, across wooded chalk escarpment. Mixture of chalk, clay and flint with several steep hills. Very mud throughout winter and spring.*
Map: *OS 1:50,000, sheet 165; 1:25,000, sheet SP 80/90.*

DESPITE the fact that the 'hardrock' areas of our fair country are considered by some the only real terrain for off-road cyclists; I can tell you from much experience that the 'softrock' South-East should not be under-estimated. In fact I'd go so far as to say that it represents the toughest going in the UK.

The Wendover area will be familiar to the many regular Jaunters who turn out each month but an intimate knowledge of the area is essential if you want to avoid upsetting anyone and having your saddle. Turn right out of Wendover station and right again at the top of the slope. Continue uphill on this road until it takes a sharp turn to the right when you'll see a track leading off to the left with the 'Ridgeway Path' sign pointing along it. When you reach the barrier take the bridleway (leftmost track) and plod on up. This is a long, gradual climb, the first few yards being a bit tricky, but it soon becomes easier. It's worth stopping for a breather by deviating out onto the grass to your right when you see the trees begin to thin, because there is a good view over the Vale of Aylesbury.

Having reached the top, when the track starts to level off a bit and veers slightly to the left, you'll see a stile in the fence ahead and here you should turn right, down a fairly steep gully. Watch out for walkers crossing (about half way down) and take care — there's a busy road at the bottom where you must make a sharp left turn, through the gate, and follow the track alongside the golf course to regain some of your elevation.

Deviate neither to left nor right until you reach road again; turn left and left again a few yards on at the junction. Just up here turn first right onto the bridleway. Taking

Overall distance : 11 miles / 17·7 Km
Road distance: 3.5 miles / 5.6 Km
Rough: 7.5 miles / 12·1 Km

Refer O/S Maps:
1: 50,000 Landranger: 165
1: 25,000 Pathfinder : SP 80/90

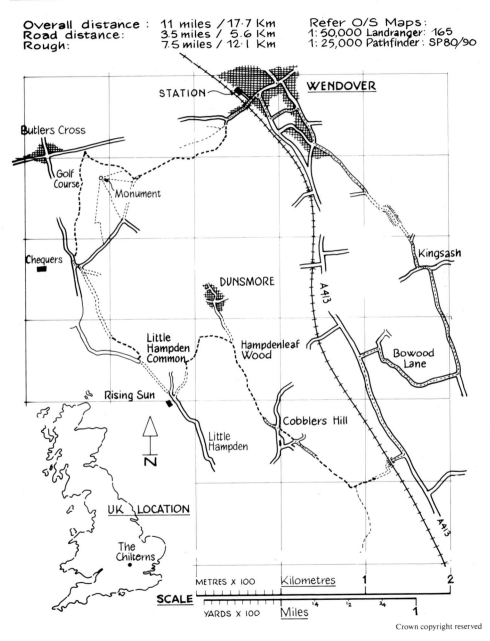

Crown copyright reserved

the lower of the two tracks, pedal on, even when it becomes a little indistinct (after a mile or so), until it joins another track at right angles where you should turn right until, after a short distance, you reach a blind lane. Turn left and continue in the direction of the lane after it ends, and across Little Hampden Common.

On emerging from the common you'll find lunch, in the shape of the Rising Sun, a little ahead and on your right.

Then take the bridleway going down at an angle into the woods opposite the pub. This is generally quite waterlogged, but firm underwheel. It takes a few slight turns as it goes downhill, but beware — there's a meggaboghole at the bottom which you will have to cross one way or another to the uphill track beyond. At the top turn right along the ridge; after rain this is a mudplugger's paradise, except for the last section, where it runs alongside a meadow.

This track soon becomes a lane, and the lane comes out onto a green; you must take the track which continues the same line, the entrance to which is not overly evident. Again, continue along the ridge — if you're going downhill, you're lost! This track joins a lane for a short way, and after this look out for a pine wood ahead. On the other side of the wood the track has a dogleg with your track heading down into the valley to the left. This downhill is best in winter because of rampant nettles in the summer; it's flinty, with a twist towards the bottom.

Go under the railway bridge and along to the end where we now embark upon the really dangerous section ... the dreaded A413 and the infernal combustion engine. After a little over half a mile, turn right into Bowood Lane.

When you come to the antique shop turn right. This is a fairly long uphill, but

being tarmac is not too uncivilised, besides which it is little used and even less maintained, thus not too unlike proper off-road.

On gaining the top of this ridge, and the junction, turn left and follow this ridgetop lane along to Kingsash where you turn left again, and, by a white house on your right, turn right into a bridleway directed to Concord. Follow this until the farm track veers off to the right and the mudbath to the left (there's a slightly easier path running parallel,on the left, beyond the bank). This is a sunken path, very popular with Jaunters, and known as Concord Gorge. It winds its way down the scarp and opens into Hogtrough Lane — a farm access lane that has happily been surfaced with half bricks.

At the end you are back in Wendover and the best return route to the station is down Dark Lane. Turn right out of Hogtrough Lane and continue uphill, past the junction on your right, and, on proceeding downhill, look out for the easily missed dark lane entrance on your left and follow it to the main road where you should turn right. When you reach the mini-roundabout turn sharp left for a cup of tea, or left proper for the station, which is up ahead a few hundred yards and down the slope to your right.

The Peddars Way (part)

Start: *Castle Acre (map ref 817 154), finish Holme next the Sea (map ref 708 431).*
Distance: *20 miles along byways, tracks and bridleways. As the going is easy, any bike with stout tyres would be suitable.*
Maps: *OS 1:50,000, sheet 132. See also The Peddars Wayt and North Norfolk Coast Path, by Bruce Robinson (HMSO)*

*and The Peddars Way leaflet from the
Planning Dept, Norfolk County Council,
Martineau Lane, Norwich NR1 2DH.*

OPENED in 1982, this is the tenth long
distance path to be approved by the
Countryside Commission. The Peddars
way, from the Latin *pes* meaning foot, is a
Roman road — the existing parts are listed
as an ancient monument — built on the
prehistoric Icknield Way. This section is
rather open and straight as are most
Roman roads and the excellence of its
construction is still evident. The Way
passes through gently undulating countryside to the dunes and salt marshes of the
coast with its bird sanctuaries and nature
reserves.

At Castle Acre it is worth visiting the
remains of the castle of William de
Warenne, son-in-law of William the
Conqueror, and especially the ruins of the
Cluniac Priory which he founded. A few
of the prior's rooms are still intact, as is
one of the finest tiers of Norman arcading
in Britain.

The bridleway and open access sections
of the 34-mile Norfolk Coastal Path from
Holme to Cromer can also be ridden.
There is also an extension of another 39
miles to Great Yarmouth. It is possible to
ride 40 miles south from Castle Acre to
Knettishall Heath near Thetford on tracks
and bridleways devised by the Norfolk
County Council for horse riders, thereby
joining with the Icknield Way and
Hereward Way.

Starting from Castle Acre, the first
stretch of the Peddars Way is a metalled
road, but after three miles it takes to the
rough. This is a lovely ride with the broad
track ahead, arrow-straight across the
farmland and with hardly a house to be
seen. The Way crosses several roads over

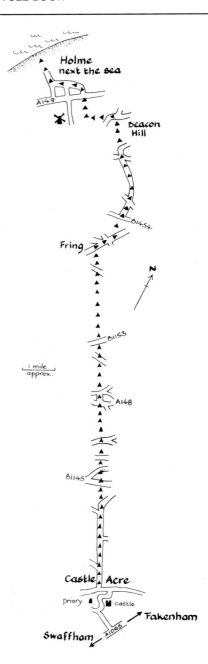

the next ten miles, but keep on until you join the road on the outskirts of Fring, where you turn right through the village and continue for a mile. Turn left on to the track by a barn and follow this to the road. Cross this and go along the road ahead for three miles, crossing two other roads, and take the bridleway as the the road turns to the right, following the Way to the top of Beacon Hill with views of the sea, dunes and marshes.

At the road, turn left then take the track to the right towards the windmill that can be seen a mile or so away. Before reaching it turn downhill into the deep stony gully which leads to the A149. Follow the road straight ahead to the T-junction, turn right and on to the beach and the Norfolk Coastal Path.

Llansantffraed Cwmdeuddwr (Mid-Wales)

Start: *Devil's Bridge or Rhayader*
Distance: *41.5 km / 25.8 miles, of which 8.5 km / 5.3 miles are along road and the remainder over the rough, comprising mountain tracks with bogs in places.*
Maps: *OS 1:50,000 sheet 147; 1:25,000 SN 87/97 & SN 86/96*

THE closest town to the start of this route is Rhayader, from where you should take the B4518, past Elan Village and the dam until, with the reservoir on your left, the road follows the headland round to the right and there is a bridge on your left across the reservoir.

Alternatively, if you want to travel to the area by train, you will need to go via Shrewsbury and Aberystwyth from where you will have to ride up to Devil's Bridge (unless you're able to bribe the guard on the train to take you up by the Vale of Rheidol line). From there take the B4343 as far as Ffair Rhos when you should take the lane going due east up to the moors.

If travelling by car park somewhere along here; continue ahead and the lane will become 'unsuitable for motor vehicles', just whatwe've been waiting for...

This track gradually drops down to run alongside the Claerwen Reservoir, where it becomes somewhat more distinct.

On reaching the dam take the road until it becomes walled or fenced and where there is an AA phonebox. At this point there is a road used as a public path veering off to your left. Take this up over the pass. Be sure to follow it round the hill to your right, towards the forest. It traverses the forset edge and enters it after about half a mile, going downhill to the bridge over the Garreg Ddu Reservoir.

This is the alternative start point to Rhayader.

Crossing the bridge, turn left and follow the road alongside the reservoir for about one and a half miles, then take the track that runs parallel to, and slightly above the road. This track takes you past one dam and follows the north side of Pen-y-Garreg Reservoir. When you come to the next dam, with the public conveniences, cross it and turn right, following the road in a westerly, then northerly direction past Hirnant.

Look out for the 'Ancient Road' doubling back to your left. This high moor route achieves a height of 542m or 1,778ft and is boggy and indistinct at times. But it is fabulous XC cycling terrain and affords spectacular views.

This section of the route is about six-and-a-half miles and you will eventually join the track that runs down into the Claerwen valley. If you came up this way then turn right for your return, or left for a return to Rhayader.

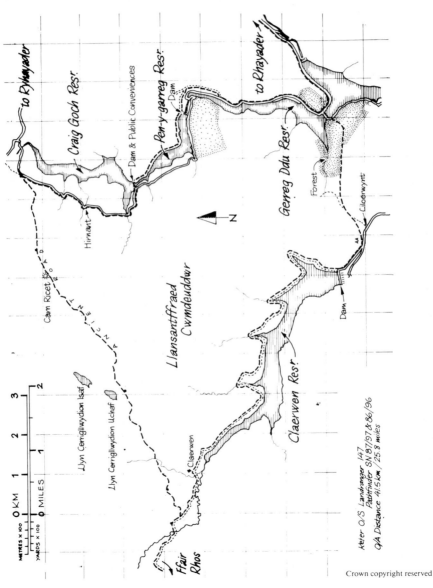

Kerer O/S Landranger 147
Pathfinder SN 87/97 & 86/96
QA Distance 41.5 km / 25.8 miles

Mid/North Wales

Start: *Llanrhaeadr or Rhyaeadr valley.*
Distance: *7 miles /11.25 km, including 2 miles along roads and the remainder over rough ground.*
Maps: *OS 1:50,000 sheet 147; 1:25,000 sheets SN 87/97 & SN 86/96.*

THIS is a short but fairly remote route. Allow three, four or even five hours if you choose it for your first high moor cycling jaunt. It was last researched fully a few years ago, so expect some changes.

Llanrhaeadr Village is reached from Oswestry on the B4580, a distance of about 13 miles. From the village take the lane signposted to Tan-y-Pistyll, Pistyll Rhaeadr or simply The Waterfall. This lane takes you up the Rhaeadr Valley and if travelling by car and not parking in the village you can park, with care, a little more than two miles along here. Just about by Maes-y-Bwch is ideal.

Continue (now cycling) along this valley lane with the Afon Rhaeadr running alongside and a remarkable abundance of varied birdlife. Take a quiet rest by the river and you'll be bound to see wagtails, and even a dipper or two. Back on the road beware, as the waterfall attracts quite a few idiots in cars, even in this remote and relatively inaccessable part of North Wales.

The lane is a steady climb and at the head of the valley is a car park, refreshments, and the big attraction — Pistyll Rhaeadr — the Waterfall. George Borrow in his book Wild Wales writes:

What shall I liken it to? I scarcely know, unless to an immense skein of silk agitated and disturbed by tempestuous blasts, or to the long tail of a grey courser at furious speed ... I never saw water falling so gracefully, so much like thin, beautiful threads as here.

The total drop is 240ft. The welsh *Pistyll Rhaeadr* means 'spout waterfall' and, indeed, about halfway down there is a level section and a kind of natural arch through which the water spouts, especially when in full flood.

Cross the little footbridge at the bottom of the falls, dismount and follow the footpath to the left. Continue on the contour; the path itself is somewhat indistinct at this stage, but with care you'll pick it up for definite as it approaches the old mine workings. Head on up the hill to your right when you reach the farmer's broad hill track which closely follows the correct course of the bridleway.

This is a hard slog, but gets the climb over fairly quickly and relatively painlessly. At the top you will have to use all your pathfinding skills because the paths on the ground seem to bear little relation to the map.

Use of the Pathfinder (1:25,000) map is recommended if you are not used to high moor navigation, and since the contour lines generally don't change, whereas other features may, they are most useful for orientation, as is a compass.

When at the top of the steep climb take the path to the left that heads along the contour in a southwesterly direction. When you've reached the back of the small tributary valley, turn left before the gate and travel alongside the fence, and, again, roughly along the contour. At this stage you'll probably think you've gone seriously wrong, and you are hopelessly lost. Look ahead; if you can see a gate (of sorts) ahead, then keep going, the path becomes much easier beyond it.

These next two miles are really most pleasant. It could be said that they represent a classic section of cross-country cycling — a long, but very gradual, remote downhill, with the odd tricky bit thrown in.

After these two miles look out for a gated and walled track on your left. Take this and continue down the twisting track until you reach Cefn-derwen where you must go through the gate to the right, down the hill, before you get to the farmhouse. Follow this track, which shortly turns into a lane just by Garwallt-fâch. This finally comes out into the valley lane hard by Maes-y-bwch.

Derbyshire Peak District

Start: *Hayfield*
Distance:*16km /10 miles, of which 3.25km/2 miles are on road and 12.75km/8 miles on rough tracks and bridleways, muddy in places.*
Maps: *OS 1:50,000 sheet 110; OS 1:25,000 sheet SK 08/18.*

IT is completely legal to ride on bridle-ways and the extensive network in this area means there is plenty of scope for longer or shorter rides. This one takes between three and four hours.

The ride starts at Brookhouse Farm, on the left as you travel north on the A624, about one-and-a-half miles out of Hayfield.

The lane we want turns off the main road where there is a slight dip, the main road going off to the right, and our lane dropping quite sharply past Brookhouse Farm, then climbing up, over a cattle-grid, towards Matleymoor Farm. It becomes a track at the point where it turns sharp left and starts a short, gradual descent to a bridleway where you should again turn left, especially if the sign says that it goes to Birch Vale.

This bridleway goes through the gate in the corner of the field and there is a short, sharp uphill ahead. Further on take the lower, more level track by the wall. The path now skirts Lantern Pike, and continues downhill, under some trees, past a house on the right, and — watch out — there's a crossroads with a minor country lane. Cross over and continue ahead and down until you reach the main road at the bottom, in Birch Vale.

Turn left, and having crossed the River Sett — about fifty yards — turn immediately right. This track soon crosses the Sett Valley Cycle Trail, based on the route of a disused railway — worth using if you are a beginner. But, for today, we cross over and head up the small path between the trees opposite. Yes this is still a bridleway, even though it goes through a park. At the top of the park there is a ramp which exits onto the A6015. Turn left here and right after about 100 yards, by some railings. You should soon pass some houses to your right and quarries to your left. The track turns fairly sharp left, and here the long gradual climb begins. Also the surface of the way degrades somewhat and becomes quite bumpy. Stick with it ... there's worse to come.

After about one-and-a-half miles of gradual climb you'll reach a crossroads, with a blind lane to the right, bridleways ahead and to the left. Take this left hand bridleway, through the gates, and brace yourself for a longish, steep and tricky climb.

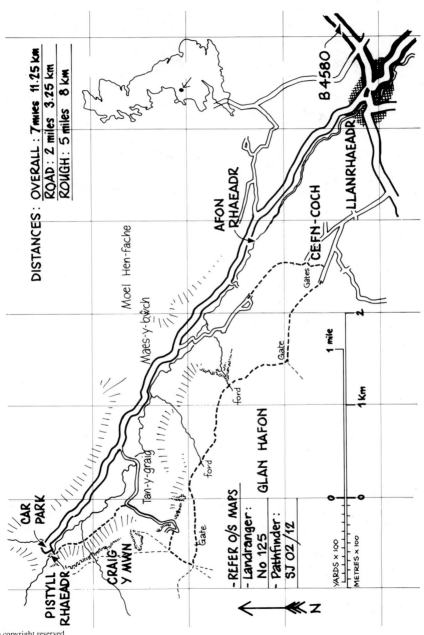

DISTANCES : OVERALL : 7 miles 11.25 km
ROAD : 2 miles 3.25 km
ROUGH : 5 miles 8 km

B 4580

AFON RHAEADR

LLANRHAEADR

CEFN-COCH

Gates

Moel Hen-fache

Maes-y-bwch

Gate

1 mile

Gate

ford

ford

1 Km

Tan-y-graig

GLAN HAFON

- REFER O/S MAPS
- Landranger :
  No 125
- Pathfinder :
  SJ 02/12

YARDS × 100
METRES × 100

N

CAR PARK

CRAIG Y MWN

Gate

PISTYLL RHAEADR

Gaining the top of the hill, turn left by the post and ride alongside the wall. The path is later flanked by a wall on both sides. This is about the half-way mark, so if the weather's fine, atop this hill is as good a place as any for a picnic.

Continue through the gates and, as the path bears to the right, look out for a signpost and take the track to your left. Now we have about a mile-and-a-half of pure downhill. After a short distance there is a path joining from the left, and at this point you should be able to see a trans-mitter mast some way straight ahead. Fork right here, and fork right again at the next junction. This is a steep, tricky downhill section following the line of Foxholes Clough.

You will have to pass through two gates before going through Phoside Farmyard. Keep right, go through the gate, and turn left down the track until you reach the main road (A624). Go straight across and up the steep road opposite. Turn left at the top. This minor road runs parallel to the main road and brings you into Hayfield without fumes. After you've crossed the river, turn right by the Post Office on your left, with a pub on your right. Continue up the hill until you see a signpost to your left for Snake Inn via William Clough. Turn up here and through the gate as the track bends to the right.

Head on along this track, through the numerous gates until you can see two small white shooting cabins ahead and a National Trust sign. Go through yet another gate and continue towards the two buildings, turning left over a footbridge before you reach them. Follow this path, along which is a challenging ford, and in due course you'll see the road ahead. Turn left onto the main road and in a very short while you'll see the lane at which this ride started.

'Summer Wine Country'

Start: *Upper Cumberworth*
Distance: *About 20 miles (32km) along green roads, tracks and other, mostly minor, roads. Going mostly good, but rough in places.*
Maps: *OS 1:50,000 sheet 110; 1:25,000 sheets SE 01/11, SE 00/10.*

THIS route around the Holme Valley involves tracks, bridleways and minor roads, some of which are part of the West Yorkshire Cycle Route.

Starting at Upper Cumberworth, between Shepley and Denby Dale at the Barnsley Road/Carr Hill Road crossroads by the Star Inn, cycle along Carr Hill Road for about 50 metres until the road bends to the right.

Turn left down Park Lane (an unsurfaced road) leading to the main road (A629) at Birdsedge. Cross over to the track opposite which soon joins a minor road, with the route bearing left along the road. At a crossroads, go straight on to the crest of a hill offering a superb view over the Holme Valley, with Holme Moss and its distinctive TV transmitter directly ahead.

Shortly after starting the descent, take the second track on the left which affords good views over New Mill. Carry straight ahead over crossroads, down a sharp descent with views across the Cheese Gate Nab. Turn right at a T-junction, descend, and at the bottom of the descent turn right at a T-junction going straight across A616, and bearing left around the village of Jackson Bridge below. The road climbs to

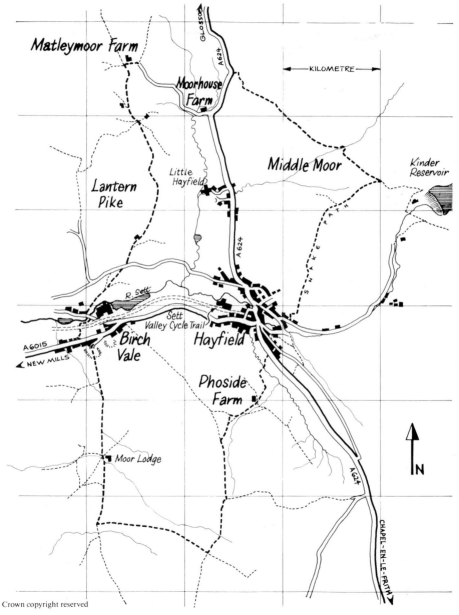

the village of Hepworth (past a mill shop).

At the junction by Hepworth Church, turn right and sharp left along Dean Lane. At the T-junction, turn right past Strines Moor Reservoir, home of the Huddersfield Sailing Club. At the T-junction with the B6106, turn right for approximately 100m, then sharp left up a track called Snittle Road. At the top of Snittle Road the route joins the West Yorkshire Cycle Route.

Turn right along the 'head of the valley' route. When this road descends, take a track off to the left called Ramsden Road. This leads down to Yateholme and Ramsden Resevoirs. At the T-junction, turn left and follow the track around the valley head until it meets the A6024. Turn right and descend into Holme Village. Turn left in the village down Fieldhead Lane. Just after passing Digley Reservoir, a picnic area is available for well earned refreshment.

Ascending Acres Lane, turn left along a bridleway called Nether Lane. Continue along until it turns sharp right back on itself (Springs Road). A feature of Springs Road is the worn stone flags where the quarry trucks have run. Go up here and

turn right onto the A635, descending to the Ford Inn. Turn left and sharp right behind the Inn onto Dean Road. At the T-junction, turn left and sharp right onto a track (Back Lane). At the end of the track, turn right for the steep descent into Holmfirth.

Turn left and cycle out of Holmfirth towards Honley on the A6024. Turn right onto a track signed to a camp site, and on reaching the A616, turn right. Next left, a sharp climb leads towards Thurstonland. Half way up, take a track on the right known as Occupation Lane, which follows the contour line. When the track ends, turn left and carry on along the minor road until you meet a T-junction just after a bend. Turn left and take the next right, and you will descend and climb a beautiful wooded valley.

Cycle through the village of Shepley, turning left at Station Road and right to join the A629. Turn left and almost immediately right, which leads onto a bridleway at the Knowle. At the T-junction, turn right along the road and next left up Heator Lane. At the junction with the A635, turn left until you reach the Star Inn (200m).

Yorkshire Dales/Settle & Carlisle Railway

Start: *Kirkby Stephen West station*
Distance: *A choice of routes of between about 25 and 35 miles (40-56kms), mostly over green roads and bridleways. Going can be very rough.*
Maps: *OS 1:50,000 sheets 91 and 98.*

THERE can be few parts in Britain so rich in tracks and byways as the limestone

country which lies mostly within North Yorkshire and goes by the loose geographical title of the 'Yorkshire Dales'.

The Roman legacy was supply routes to outposts built to keep an eye on the Brigantes and police the mining of lead in these hills.

The growth of the lead industry in the early years of the Industrial Revolution led to the laying of a new network of trade routes, while the Dales were already criss-crossed by ancient packhorse routes in the

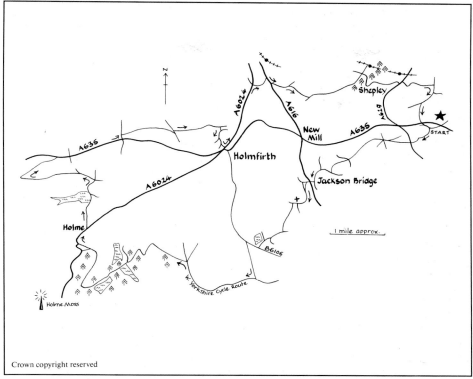

days when Daniel Defoe was setting a futuristic style for documentary travel writing. Add a goodly mesh of drove roads, bridleways, quarrymen's and other traders' paths and the off-road rider is well and truly spoilt for choice.

There is another bonus which gives the Dales one up on other comparable uplands as far as the cyclist is concerned — the Settle & Carlisle railway can get you and your bike speedily to the very heart of the hills.

Although at the time of writing the long-term future of this route along the back-bone of England remained subject to a ministerial decision, the indications were that even Government sanction for its

closure by British Rail would not result in an immediate end to services. So this route assumes you'll still be able to catch the morning train to Kirkby Stephen for a good while yet.

The following provides a basic route starting at Kirkby Stephen and returning from a choice of stations to the south. Kirkby Stephen station is some distance west of the town and about 350ft above it, but the town has a fine church, and several pubs and cafes if you fancy the detour. If joining the route from Kirkby Stephen town you should backtrack along the station road until the road bears right just after the bridge crossing a disused railway, where you should take lane which forks

75

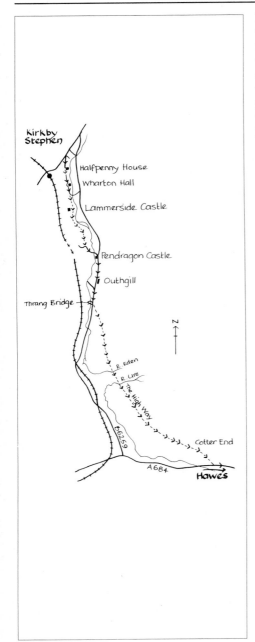

left to Halfpenny House. If coming from the station, be prepared for a sharp right at the foot of the hill as you come into the town. After Halfpenny House the route continues by way of a track and bridleway to Wharton Hall, a fortified house dating from the 14th century. The route continues, following the line of the River Eden and passing the ruined Lammerside Castle before it joins a metalled by-road where a left turn brings you past another castle, Pendragon, which legend has it was the birth place of King Arthur.

The castle was last restored and lived in by Lady Anne Clifford and it is a route sometimes known as Lady Anne Clifford's Way that we shall now follow.

Join the B6259 a few yards from the castle and continue through the tiny settlement of Outhgill. About three quarters of a mile beyond this a track goes down to the right, crossing the river at Thrang Bridge. Ignore this, but turn left after a few yards by way of the green road that bears up the hillside. This is the ancient Highway which dates from the Bronze Age and was used by Lady Anne Clifford almost 400 years ago on her journeys from Skipton to her castles at Pendragon, Brough and Appleby.

The Highway follows the edge of the escarpment past the headwaters of the Eden, flowing towards the Irish Sea, and into the head of Wensleydale, home of the River Ure which flows to the North Sea. The road is rough and muddy in parts, particularly on the descent down Cotter End where you join the main A684 to Hawes, soon passing the reputedly haunted Rigg House on your left.

Hawes is well endowed with shops, cafes pubs, and a museum, while a detour via Hardraw will bring a chance to see the highest single-drop waterfall in England in

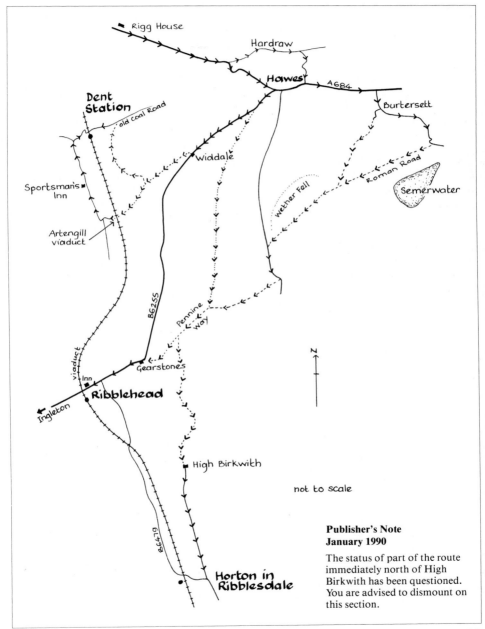

not to scale

Publisher's Note
January 1990

The status of part of the route immediately north of High Birkwith has been questioned. You are advised to dismount on this section.

77

the grounds of the Green Dragon Hotel.

From Hawes a variety of routes will return the rider to a choice of stations. To return to Dent station — at 1,150ft the highest main line station in England — take the Ingleton road from Hawes for about three miles until you see Widdale chapel and a phone box on the left. At the crossroads immediately before this, turn right and keep to the lower track. This green road leads up over the fell and eventually passes beneath the fine Artengill viaduct. Turn right, past the Sportsman's Inn, then right again to reach the station up its steep zigzag bank. Alternatively look for the rough bridleway which goes off to the right just after the summit of the pass and follows the countour to the old Coal Road, a mile above the station (turn left).

For Ribblehead and Horton-in-Ribblesdale stations, take the green road which bears away up the fellside on a right bend a mile out of Hawes. On the summit plateau this joins the Roman road which at this point forms part of the Pennine Way. Follow the road down the fellside and where it levels out, a right fork leads you to Gearstones and, turning left along the road, to Ribblehead station with its pub and famous 24-arch viaduct. Note that only southbound trains stop here as there is only one platform.

A left fork takes you through undulating drumlin country to High Birkwith farm and the road to Horton which has a pub and a popular walkers' cafe.

Alternatively, for view over Semerwater, head east along the A684 from Hawes, taking the second right, through Burtersett. At the head of the village turn right past the institute and first left by the track which leads via the saddle between Yorburgh and Wether Fell — a popular hang gliding site — to the Roman road (turn right). For a less arduous climb, keep to the 'main' road through Burtersett and, after a mile, join the Roman road, on your right, at a hairpin.

The routes described in this chapter were supplied by various contributors — the Quantocks, North Downs, Chilterns, two Welsh routes and the Peak District routes were drafted by Geoff Apps and first published by Making Tracks magazine; the North and South Downs Way, the Downs Link and the Peddars Way were written by David Wrath-Sharman, Summer Wine Country by Richard Feast, and the Dales route by Stan Abbott.

The publishers strongly recommend the use of an appropriate Ordnance Survey map or guide book.

Chapter Nine

Survival Servicing

by Dave Wrath-Sharman

LET'S face it, whatever bike you have, be it rough stuff, mountain or a custom made cross-country cycle, if you ride across country it's going to get in a mess. Fine abrasive dust on dry summer days, thick glutinous mud in winter, and all shades in between will take their toll. Parts will wear out and break. You can't avoid it, but you can minimise it.

So what can you do? Firstly ride in a sensitive and sensible manner. If you hammer along, thumping and bumping over ruts and rocks, don't be surprised if you get loose spokes, damaged rims, split and cut tyres — never mind the damage to your wrists and back. Learn to ride your bike well, how to help it over the bumps and minimise the impact on your bike and on you (and on the countryside). Ask an experienced rider to show you the ropes.

There are several people who organise training weekends for beginners and master classes for more advanced riders.

You can do a lot to save wear and tear just by learning to read the terrain, pick your way and avoid the worst bits. Don't wallow through mud unnecessarily, unless of course, wallowing in mud baths is your thing. But then, you know the score, so you won't go moaning to your cycle shop that the chain/rings/sprocket only lasted three months and that the freewheel sounds like a cement mixer. (What were those funny little brown things in there anyway....?) Riding your bike skilfully and looking after it can actually be more fun and more rewarding (and cheaper) than ploughing through everything in sight.

But even if you take responsibility for the way you ride, your bike will still get in a mess and parts will still break. So let's look at some of the reasons why, so you can do something about it. Many people have bought mountain bikes or cross-country cycles because of the 'tough' image. They see them as low-maintenance, indestructible machines able to bomb about town and country with impunity.

Around town that is largely true. Wheels and tyres will take a lot of punishment and the frames are more robust than those of road bikes, but in the country it's a slightly different story. Many of the components are the same as those on road bikes though usually of a higher quality. Even where components are specially designed and made for the job, there are still many levels of excellence; some do the job better, some are stronger than others, and this is nearly always related to price. All components and all bikes are compromises; the manufacturer has an unenviable job balancing the price/performance equation when working out specifications.

Not everybody will be suited by a

particular specification. Some people only want to ride an easy bridleway on a summer's day, some will want to race down one of those one-in-four Welsh firebreaks at fifty miles an hour, while others of my acquaintance aren't happy unless they're exploring in the bleakest country and in the worst weather conditions with full panniers. Obviously, what would suit the bridleway rider may be inadequate for the firebreak specialist,and what would be a good bike for him wouldn't do at all for our Dr Livingston (presumably) and what would be perfect for the good doctor would be completely over the top for our easy rider.

A bike is a highly personal piece of equipment. Only you, the rider, really know what you want your bike for, so — as you will be advised in Chapter 11 — choose it very carefully, and don't be swayed by fashion. Many bridleway riders would be better suited by a good quality touring bike fitted with heavy tyres, than a mountain bike. If cost is a limiting factor be even more careful: don't expect the manufacturer to have got everything perfect for you. If it doesn't perform well enough for your needs, change it. Set it up for yourself, rework it to fit your purpose, weight and style. If any component breaks or proves unreliable, don't automatically blame the manufacturer or shop — you may simply be asking too much of it. But whatever else you do, replace it with a better/higher specification component as soon as you become aware of the problem. If you don't, you can't complain when it lets you down again — and it will. Don't expect top range performance from bottom range prices; remember the old adage 'you get what you pay for'.

A word of caution here: just because you've paid a lot doesn't necessarily mean the component can do the job. The Huret Duopar rear derailleur was a case in point. It is a truly wonderful gear changer, beloved by tourists everywere for its ability to handle super-wide ratio gears.

For this reason it was fitted to several cross-country machines, as they also use very wide ratios. But the requirements of a jolting, jarring cross-country bike is totally different to the road machine for which it was designed. The changer proved too light and flexible for these conditions and couldn't control the chain, which would jump off the pulleys and jam in the cage. The result was not pretty or useable. One loyal fellow broke three of these on his cross-country cycle before he bowed to the inevitable and bought a derailleur designed for the job. He wouldn't use anything other than a Titanium Duopar on his road bike of course.

Rear derailleur mechanisms, particularly those of the long arm type, are the most vulnerable item on a cross-country bike. They are prone to catch on rocks and logs often as a result of the rider's lack of awareness. The great majority of failed derailleurs I've seen and heard of, were broken by the rider insisting on changing gear when applying maximum welly. I watched one chap attempt to jump three cogs at once while trying to climb a steep muddy gully — needless to say the operation was terminal. No derailleur, no matter how strong, will stand up to such treatment for long. So if you've broken a few, don't keep blaming the derailleur, go for the cause. Look at your gear changing technique, you may find you're trying to change gear too late.

You are going to need some basic skills and knowledge if you intend doing a lot of cross-country riding, especially if you ride on your own. I'm not going to tell you how to dismantle or adjust your bike in this chapter. If you don't know enough to look after your bike, or do the little jobs I'm suggesting, get someone to show you, and invest in a good cycle maintenance book such as Richard's Bicycle Book.

One of the first 'customising' jobs I would do on any bike is to dismantle the headset, bottom bracket bearings, and the wheel bearings too, if you've got the adjustable cone type. Clean with a solvent like Gunk or Jizer, NOT paraffin (or petrol — it's too dangerous) then repack with a good waterproof grease. The best one for cross-country work is available from trials motorcycle shops and is made by Bel-Ray. This is even salt-waterproof and seems to be a close cousin to contact adhesive! Great stuff, but it has one drawback — it tends to get rather stiff in very cold weather. There is another specialist grease available from motor cycle shops known as Slick 50. It's a synthetic Teflon-based lubricant able to handle temperatures from -20°F (-29°C) to 500°F (310°C). It is good in all bearings, especially freewheels. Another Bel Ray product is racing chain lube. It's wonderful in the new oil-ported free-wheels but do not use it on your chain — it's too sticky by far. These special lubes really are effective in protecting your bearings against water.

'Sealed' wheel bearings are a bit of a problem as the seal isn't total, despite claims commonly made by mountain bike manufacturers. They are reasonably effective if they truly are the sealed type, and these can be recognised by the rubber membrane covering the ball bearings. If they have a metal diaphragm then they are simply shielded against dust. The main purpose of seals and shields is to keep grease in the bearing. Both these bearing types would benefit from the waterproof grease treatment. The bearings must be removed from their housings, then the inside seal (if fitted) can be gently prised out with a sharp implement. Clean thoroughly to remove all traces of ordinary grease, repack with waterproof grease and refit. Sealed bearings are able to keep out water unless pressure, such as a jet spray, or a head of water is involved, as it would be in a deep river crossing. Once water gets in, they are unable to drain and will need to be dismantled or replaced.

So what else can you do to help your bike to survive the rigours of cross-country work? At the risk of stating the obvious, look after it. Clean and lubricate your bike as soon after your ride as you can. All it takes is common sense, and yet I know many riders who don't look at their bikes, let alone clean them in between rides. They display the caked-on muck like a badge of office in an attempt to 'look the part'. (Why clean cross country bikes — they only get dirty again don't they?) Yet these same people always seem to be fiddling with their bikes, keeping their friends waiting, often the first to moan that their bikes are always letting them down, that nothing seems to last, ad nauseam.

Cleaning isn't just a case of removing surface muck for cosmetic reasons — it's an opportunity for close-up inspection.

Cleaning a cross-country bike after a muddy winter ride is a chore, but it needn't take long if done straight away while the bike is still wet. I find the best way is to use a low pressure water hose to get the worst off, using a 25mm paint brush at the same time for the twiddly bits.

Some people use the type of high pressure jet cleaner found on garage forecourts. Very effective, but also good at forcing grit and water into wheel bearings and freewheels unless used very carefully. Use the hose and brush on the chain, running it backwards until you're sure it is free of grit. I never recommend using oil on the chain of a bike used across country. Oil picks up too much grit and dust and needs to be cleaned off with solvents, which get inside the chain (taking fine grit with them) and making effective relubrication difficult. Better to use the synthetic PTFE-based*(polytetrafluoroethylene)* lubricants like Tri-Flon or Superspray Lube which, incidentally, uses carbon dioxide as a propellant — not ozone damaging fluorocarbons. These are 'dry film' lubricants and therefore pick up little grit. The waxy lubes like LPS 3 or Bikegard 3 are also very good, but are not as 'dry' as the others. You should be aware that all these synthetic oils and greases .are not compatible with normal mineral oil-based lubricants: use one type or the other — together they will emulsify. Even synthetics will get washed off in very harsh wet conditions, but they leave a thin lubricating film on the chain so don't lose their effectiveness. They all displace water, so reapplication is no problem.

The fact that these can be washed off the

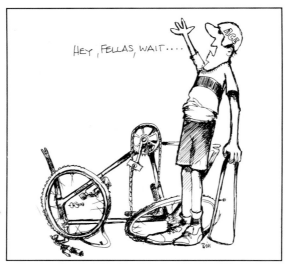

HEY, FELLAS, WAIT....

...fiddling with their bikes, keeping their friends waiting...

surface of the chain with water is an advantage; it means you can get the grit off the outside without disturbing the lube inside the chain. So, if the chain is really caked with mud, remove it from the bike and clean it under a hot water tap. After cleaning, dry off in an a low oven or over a radiator and then liberally lubricate while still warm. When the carrier has evaporated, wipe off the excess. Make sure the chainwheels and sprockets are free of gunge — you will probably need a degreaser — before refitting the clean chain. Relubricate your chain often.

After thoroughly cleaning the bike treat all external moving parts with a water displacing penetrating spray like WD 40 or LPS 1. Make sure you get the spray into the derailleur mechanisms and gear and brake lever pivots. When lubricating the brake arm pivots be careful not to get it onto the brake blocks or rims; if you do, clean off with trichloroethylene or alcohol. If you have hub brakes you can spray the rims with advantage, particularly in the spoke holes, but be very careful around the backplates; if you get any lubricant on hub brake shoes they must be replaced.

Keep a close watch on the brake blocks;

they can wear very quickly in bad weather. If they become misaligned they can cut the sidewalls, especially if wide tyres are used on narrow rims. Turn the blocks round before they get too badly worn. Check the braking surfaces of the rims from time to time; they can get dangerously thin and then distort in an emergency, or flatten if they 'bottom out' on a tree root. I wonder if tracks and bridleways one hundred years hence will be coloured a shiny silver grey?

The wheels of mountain bikes and cross-country cycles are very tough, using heavy rims and fat tyres, but you still need to keep an eye on spoke tension and rim truth (your brakes depend on it). Learn to tension spokes and true a wheel yourself. It's not difficult — get someone to show you or consult a maintenance manual, like Richard's Bicycle Book. Edinburgh Cycle Shop has even produced a good video demonstrating the technique. Perhaps you won't do a wonderful job at first but practice makes perfect and you may be glad of the skill one day when you're miles away from anywhere.

Check your tyres for cuts often. If you habitually use low pressures and especially if a ripple is showing in the side wall (too low), examine for splits or broken threads. If you find any, replace the tyre immediately. Don't try and make do — it will let you down at the worst possible time. Many fat tyres are fitted with undersized inner tubes, so the tube is stretched when inflated. These puncture more easily than those fitted with proper full size tubes, so replace them. You could also try the various tyre sealants, although I've not found them reliable enough myself. They undoubtedly work for trials motor cycles, but with our smaller diameter tyres there probably isn't sufficient volume of air for consistent results and you often have to be

pump the tyre up several times to get a proper seal. In very wet conditions when a sealant would be most appreciated they are even less reliable.

It is under these very conditions that punctures are most annoying and difficult to repair. So I'm going to tell you how to do it properly. Most writers on the subject always assume fair weather and plenty of time, but life's not always like that. So here we are — a wet day, a sea of mud and failing light. For starters, why haven't you got a spare? OK, so you lent it to your friend. (Where was his/hers?)

Two things, and two things only are important when repairing a puncture. The tube must be absolutely **clean** and **dry** if the patch is to stick. Try and clean the tyre and rim first if it's wet and muddy, then get the the tube out, all of it, and dry that too. First, feel round the inside of the tyre for the culprit and remove it — note the location in relation to the valve to give you a guide of where to look. Pump up the tube so it's well stretched and inspect it inch by inch. Listen for the leak, feel for it with your lips and pinpoint it with the tip of your tongue. If you can't find it, pump the tube up to a higher pressure, then when it reveals itself, mark it using a felt-tipped pen. Don't let the tube down yet (it should be about the size it will be in the tyre). You now need to clean the area of the puncture thoroughly; that scruffy bit of sandpaper isn't much use at the best of times, but is totally useless in the wet! Use the edge of a sharp knife to scrape the tube clean; there should be a film of rubber on the blade if done properly. This will ensure the tube is dry too. Don't let it down yet. Now apply a little solution to the leak, quickly smear it out just a little bigger than the patch you're going to use.

Now let the solution dry completely; if

it's not, the patch won't stick, so don't try and rush it. Peel a patch and stick it onto the still inflated tube, press it in place with your thumb, keep the pressure on and now let the tube down. Still keep pressing with your thumb for a couple of minutes; you're also warming the patch which helps it to stick.

The advantage of this method is that the patch is relaxed when inflated in the tyre; quite important with big tyres. If the leak is so big that you can't keep the tyre inflated, then use the biggest patch you have and let it cure for longer, say five minutes. Always check again for leaks and thorns before refitting the tyre.

Brake and gear cables don't need much looking after, but do check for broken strands. If you find any, replace them straight away; you can't afford to have them break. Always upgrade to the best when replacing cables; nothing less than 1.5 braided cables with Teflon lined outers will do. Carefully cut the cable with really sharp pliers or cable cutters, 25mm longer than required. Warm up the end with a soldering iron, and dip into Bakers Fluid (flux) to clean it, then tin with solder for about 50mm and wipe off any excess with a rag while the solder is still molten. The advantage of this method is that the clamp bolt tightens onto the soldered section of the cable; it won't slip or fray and will last much longer. Never oil or grease Teflon-lined cables.

So you've learnt how to ride sensibly and altered and tuned your bike to suit. You clean and lubricate your bike religiously after every ride, and repair or replace anything that goes wrong straight away. You think you've done every thing you can — you think nothing can go wrong now? Don't you believe it!

You will never see a contract that says 'This person has done all they can — fate will agree to leave them alone'. Life just isn't like that — you need to develop the Belt and Braces philosophy. Always carry tools and spares.

A tool kit needn't be heavy but it does need to be carefully considered. You'll need a good quality 6" adjustable spanner for wheels and all small nuts. I wouldn't bother with a dumbell spanner — they break. With some bikes you'll only need to carry two or three Allen keys. If your bike has adjustable bearings you'll need a cone spanner, which can be cut down, a small screwdriver and maybe a small pair of pliers capable of cutting cable. A chain rivet extractor is vital; if your derailleur breaks you can remove it and then shorten the chain for a single gear. Carry a crank remover and a suitable socket spanner. Some cranks now have a self-contained extractor built in, a 'one-key release', which really works. There's not much point in carrying a freewheel block remover. I've never found anyone who can remove a block without the aid of a bench vice after they've been wound on with sub-20" gears! Fit a good sealed freewheel instead. A spoke key — machined not pressed — a set of plastic tyre levers and a good sharp folding knife just about rounds up the tools.

The spares you need depend a lot on your bike, but I'd suggest the following:

- Puncture repair outfit comprising solution, patches (the nice feather-edged ones), a felt tipped pen and rubberised canvas or a piece of old tyre with the bead removed to repair a split tyre.
- A tube of waterproof grease and selection of ball bearings.
- Rear gear and brake inner cables — use for the front brake and derailleur too, cut

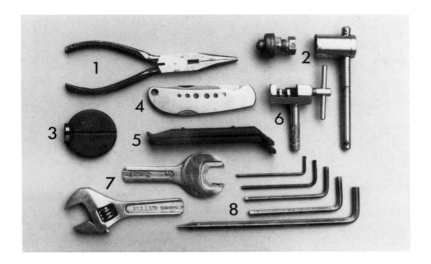

GOING PREPARED — above, basic tool kit: 1 pliers, 2 crank extractor and box spanner for same, 3 spoke key, 4 knife, 5 tyre levers, 6 chain link separator, 7 adjustable and cone spanners, 8 Allen keys.

Below, emergency repair kit:1 spokes, 2 rubber bands, copper wire and nylon cord, 3 insulation tape, 4 valves, 5 chain links, 6 assorted nuts and bolts, 7 felt pen and puncture repair kit, 8 assorted ball bearings, spare cable inners and pot of grease, 9 inner tube.

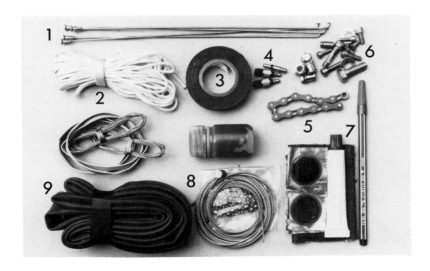

85

or roll up the excess.

- Carry a few spokes and nipples; unforeseen accidents can happen to even the strongest wheels.
- Modern chains rarely break, but I've seen it happen, so carry a short length of used chain; it's no good fitting a new bit in an old chain.
- A brake cable clamp bolt or solderless nipple if you use hub brakes and a few nuts and bolts, like chainring bolts and pannier or mudguard bolts appropriate to your bike.

A length of strong string, some thin wire and rubber bands cut from an old inner tube are really handy. I did a temporary repair to one chap's cantilever brake after the return spring had broken. He commented 'wasn't it lucky' I was carrying that sort of stuff. It struck me as funny how some people see deliberate forethought as 'luck'!

Some strong insulating tape is a must too. I've seen a friend use insulating tape and an adjustable spanner to hold together a broken rear dropout. He clamped the spanner on to the axle with the wheel nut and bound the handle to the chain stay with the tape — it got him home!

We've been thinking about your bike, but I'd also ask you to consider the things that can go wrong with yourself. Carry a first aid kit and basic survival kit and know how to use them. Don't be tempted to ride alone until you're very experienced in all aspects of cross country cycling. You can never be too well prepared — maintenance and skill will not prevent accidents, but I hope after reading this you're able to spend more of your time riding.

Chapter Ten

Pinnacles of Achievement

Tales of two mountains to give us all something to aspire to

More a walk than a ride

One mile high (well, nearly)

LIKE all appallingly bad ideas, this one was hatched over several glasses of beer. And like all bad ideas, it seemed like a good idea at the time.

In truth, the idea of a bike ride up Ben Nevis had been fermenting in my mind for some months. I had been riding a mountain bike regularly for some time but felt the need to push myself and my machine a little further. In short, I was looking for a challenge and Ben Nevis seemed to offer just that. A fairly naff challenge I freely admit — after all, people have driven cars up Ben Nevis, roller skated up Ben Nevis, ski-ed up Ben Nevis, and a host of other things up Ben Nevis. Indeed, that august lump of Scottish rock has suffered more fund-raising daft ideas than even Bob Geldof could handle. Still, there it was. It was Ben Nevis or bust.

Ah, there's the rub. Accepting or issuing challenges to myself is all well and good but most of them I never seem to get round to actually doing. The justifications are various: the I-would-have-done-but-it-was-just-not-convenient-at-the-time solution is the most frequent. Somehow, I had to make sure that this was one challenge I did not back out of.

Two factors conspired to make the Ben Nevis trip a cert. Firstly, my family were (and are still) greatly involved in the local fell search and rescue team, so much so that the team's Landrover ambulance is a permanent resident at our house. Secondly, the said ambulance had long outlived its useful life and the team could not afford to buy a new one. The solution was therefore obvious — make my ride up the Ben a sponsored event with all monies going to the Landrover Appeal. That way I could not back out.

The enthusiasm with which the idea was received was flattering and not a little unnerving. Obviously, the fundraising committee had to be consulted first and approval granted. This was promptly done — but with one proviso. One of the committee members, Cliff Sore, had to do the ride with me. Indeed, he absolutely insisted on it!

I had known Cliff for a while. Late 30s, fit, a keen cyclist and not a little competitive. With him breathing down my neck there would be no backing out without considerable loss of face, and with the full weight of the team behind us the idea was quite prosposterous anyway. From that point on, Bikes up Ben Nevis was all systems go.

I already had a 1:25,000 inch map of Ben Nevis and felt I knew the mountain like the back of my hand by the time Cliff and I came to discuss routes and plans for the trip. I had already discovered that the easiest way up was by Coire Leis rather than by the tourist track from Glen Nevis. Both led up to the shoulder of the mountain at about 2,000ft but the Coire Leis route had gradients which looked more feasible for mountain biking. Neither of us had been up the Ben before so we were relying totally on the map at this stage. On the face of it, my route looked the most logical and we agreed that this would be our initial means of access onto the mountain.

The rescue team offered full back-up so it was arranged that a number of team members would come with us on the ride, to provide support, guidance and (God forbid) help if the going got really tough.

I had been watching the weather forecasts quite closely in the weeks before the ride. It was not promising. Phone calls to Nevisport, an outdoor shop in Fort William which normally has a good idea of the conditions prevailing on the Ben, revealed that there was still a great deal of snow on the summit. For all it was the middle of May, the snowline was a good 350ft below the summit plateau with fresh snow falling all the time. The day before we set off for Scotland, a further phone call suggested that the conditions had worsened slightly and ice axes were being recommended. Clearly, this was going to be no picnic.

It was the May Bank Holiday weekend. Cliff and I, plus two other team members, set off on the Friday evening. Our intention was to camp in Glen Nevis with the rest of the team arriving later with the bikes. It was a fine evening for a drive into Scotland but by the time we had reached Fort William it was blowing a gale and

raining in sheets, with every appearance of it continuing to do so for the next 72 hours. This was precisely what we did not need.

The support crew had been locked out of the campsite (having arrived well after midnight) and so spent the night trying to coax some sleep in a rather cramped Transit van. We all awoke to quite diabolical weather. A party was sent to the police station at Fort William for a weather forecast and also to inform them of our presence. The forecast was not good — a temporary respite in the storm before becoming even worse. Today was Saturday; we had to return home on Sunday. A hurried team meeting in the Transit agreed that Cliff and I had to make the attempt today at around lunchtime when the respite was expected.

The bikes were assembled and checked. An advance party set off for the summit at 11.30. Cliff and I would be taken in the Transit to sea level near Corpach and begin the ride from there while another group would head for the shoulder and meet us half-way. We loaded the minibus and, in blinding rain, set off for the shores of Loch Linnhe. A hurried photo on the sands and then on the bikes for the mile or so along the main road to the golf course and our route up into Coire Leis.

It was a relief to be riding at last and sure enough, the weather broke slightly as we crossed the immaculately kept greens of Fort William Golf Club en route for Coire Leis. We rode and carried up the first steep section from the golf course to the lip of the coire and with the jagged cliffs of the Ben visible at last we began to ride in earnest. The going was tougher than expected, the ground being little more than a porridge-like mixture of peat and water. We were either up to our axles in the stuff or sliding around, back wheels spinning like crazy trying to gain purchase. We passed a group of walkers heading out of the coire — bad weather had forced them to abort their climb to the summit and they were heading back to Fort William. The weather couldn't be that bad on top, could it? Cliff and I pressed on.

Three quarters of the way up the coire we rested before crossing the burn onto the flanks of Nevis itself. Here the ground conditions improved — drier, rockier but more technical. We expected this to be the easiest part of the climb but it was still more difficult than we had predicted. We had been in radio contact with the shoulder party for a while but now we could see them clearly. Cliff and I had tremendous thirsts and so were well pleased when we found the party huddled behind a boulder with a brew on.

We didn't rest for long, it was too cold. The shoulder party split, some returning to base, the rest escorting us up to the summit. But first we had the zig-zags to negotiate. This is the steepest part of the mountain and for more than 1,000ft it was all but impossible to ride. Bikes around our necks, we headed into the gale and upwards towards the summit.

The cloud had been lifting all afternoon but it was still down to around 3,000ft. Just as the steep zig-zags began to really bite into our energy reserves we lost sight of everything below. We were in thick cloud now and the patches of deep snow gave way to a dull white snowfield stretching up into the gloom. Pete Roberts was leading. Conversation had dropped to a bare minimum and I concentrated instead on the ice axe hanging from the back of his rucksack.

We passed another climber on the way back. Pete had a few words with him but refused to tell us what he had said. Just as

well, I thought. The conditions had become scary enough without knowing exactly how dangerous they were.

Suddenly, the snow field levelled out. The summit plateau at last! Back on the bikes, we tried to cycle the last few hundred yards to the summit cairn. It was well below freezing and the gale was blowing at around 50mph. We spotted a snow cornice jutting out over the cliffs and steered well clear. One foot on that and it was 1,500ft straight back down into Coire Leis.

The summit party had taken over the tiny shelter on the summit and the Primus was going full tilt. Everything, including the bikes, was encrusted with ice and it was difficult to believe that this was high summer. We took shelter, drank tea made from the snows of Ben Nevis and posed for photographs around the trig point. Cliff and I were exhausted, elated and very cold..

Now, all we had to do was get down! And that proved to be just as challenging as the climb!

Iain Lynn

At the summit

89

Bicycles up Kilimanjaro

I TOOK a deep breath of anticipation and bent over to grab the chunky black handlebar grip, then getting a firm grasp with my other hand on the well-sprung B22 saddle, I started to break my bike free of the snow. This was the start of a very long arduous day. We were already 18,500ft above sea-level. It was frighteningly cold and the air was thin, dry and hard.

We were wrapped from head to toe as a barrier against frost bite and ultra-violet light. Snow goggles were indispensable. We had flown 3,000 miles and climbed for five days to get here and now we were within striking distance of the summit of the highest mountain in Africa. Ahead of us was a long icy ridge. The summit looked close but it was over a mile distant. No-one had ever ridden bicycles this high. Would it be possible? Could we do it? Would the bikes survive?

I pulled my bicycle upright and staightened my back. The handlebars looked cold and angular: ready for a tussle. I glanced at the pedals: mean rat-traps clammering for a real test and straining for a turn of power. My legs felt weak already. I tightened the drawstrings on my waist and tucked in the cuffs of my gloves. A cold shiver ran up my spine. I sighed.

'Come on, you Dick,' shouted cousin Nick. He was already climbing on his bike. I bounced my machine to knock off the snow, then wriggled my shoulders to get the rucksack comfortable before hoisting my leg over the saddle. By the time I looked up, Nick was sprawled on the ground. Downer Number One of The Bicycle Summit Bid. The bike was out of sight. Nick rolled over five feet from me,

sat up and burst into laughter: 'Crazy start to a cycling epic. My ice axe slipped off my cross bar and caught between my legs, tripped me up and the bike escaped over that icy boulder. Let's find out the damage.'

There was no damage. We lifted both bikes over the next couple of boulders and sat down for a rest. Our hearts were pounding as we tried to gasp the oxygen in the thin air. Altitude sickness was weighing heavy with thumping headaches, nausea, and eye irritation from the bright light reflecting off the snows. Dehydration would be a problem later as the low air pressure dried our lungs out quickly. We only had two pints of water for the day. The temperature hovered around -10°C. It was New Year's Eve.

The low morning sun cut diagonally into the crater of Kilimanjaro. We aimed to traverse the volcanic rim as it rose from here along jagged black spires interlaced with snow. Then to the rounded ice slopes leading up to the summit plateau itself. The highest point, soaring way above the clouds, is called Uhuru Peak. At 19,347ft it's on top of the world: an island of sanity standing above precipitous crags rimmed by snow cornices and plunging several hundreds of feet vertically down into the crater. The outer slopes of the volcano are violent and ice-clad, punctuated by ice seracs and lava buttresses. No place to go mending bicycle punctures!

We got up and cycled on — this time more cautiously than before. We pedalled smoothly up gentle inclines and halted breathless at the crests. We descended short slopes with bums raised from the saddle, hanging out backwards with brakes squeezing on. The knobbly two-and-a half-inch diameter tyres which had performed so admirably in the gooey mud 10,000ft below, had a tenacious grip on the firm snow crust. The ultra-low gear combination went down to an 18-inch bottom which allowed us to climb anything where we could get the traction.

After four taxing hours, half way to Uhuru Peak, a short snow slope had us beaten. We collapsed exhausted and had to carry the bikes to the top of the rise. From there we gazed with excitement down an impressive 20-yard run with glistening snow slopes disappearing off both sides. 'Action,' we yelled enthusiastically and leapt on our bikes, starting excellently with a push off from a gigantic icicle.

Our bikes rolled easily for ten yards and we pedalled over a hunch-back cornice. We turned a tight left hand corner which had been out of sight and I saw Nick's back wheel hang out a drop too far. A flush of powder snow filled the air then he corrected quickly up front. This brought the bike upright again as his left foot went down to touch the snow and a curse went up. But the trailing foot unbalanced him. The front wheel slewed off to the right and Nick's left leg crumpled.

Before I knew it, snow was everywhere. Knobbly tyres jumped up and then twisted and disappeared. A light blue anorak spun over to reveal dark dungarees. An Intermediate Technology banner stuck up momentarily and then flashed away. A hand, a boot and a yell flicked out from a ball of fun before all rushed off spinning down the slope.

A second later, I noticed a frigid ice wall tens of feet below, then, too late, saw the sheet of ice under my own racing wheels. My brakes were helplessly locked on. First: tyres teased the snow. In an instant I was on my knees and then my bum. I spun round, rolled over and careered into Nick.

A long drawn-out moment of silence:

Richard, left, and Nick on the summit plateau

possibly ten minutes, but probably ten seconds. One word from Nick: 'Bummer.'

And then: 'Technical misjudgement.'

'Corner Grade 3C veering to Grade 4B,' I added, spitting snow out of my mouth and raising myself on my elbows.

A second later we exploded in laughter: a couple of fools sliding around with bicycles in the snow at nearly 20,000ft on New Year's Eve. This is the essence and beauty of mountain biking. We looked at each other through serious dark snow goggles and creased up again. We were full of ourselves, jubilant with our imminent success, bubbling over with adrenalin and excitement.

We laughed so much that next minute we were heaving with breathlessness, sucking at thin air, chests arching skywards, like

At the roof of the world, Richard, the writer, is on the left

Yeti involved in a nuptual embrace. Squeezing a bellyaching laugh between lung-stretching gasps for energy.

It took a while to calm ourselves down. The time was noon and we had another 500ft to cycle to the summit plateau before we could retreat to safety. Once we had re-established a more moderate state of breathing, and calmed our heartrates to nearer normal, we could start to pick ouselves up.

I screwed the snow out of my ears. Nick brushed his face down, cold snow dropped down my neck: tantalising like the fingers of an ice maiden, though luckily not as agonising as a frozen bike pump up your trouser leg.

I stood up first. All limbs still in place. No clothes torn. Nick likewise. We had spun free from the bikes, but they were locked in a loving embrace. Romeo had his pedal through Juliet's spokes. Juliet had wrapped her bars around Romeo's saddle. Cables entwined.

Nick dusted down Romeo's derailleur. I grabbed Juliet by the rear end and hauled her upright. Spun the wheels. Still true. Brakes free, but handlebars twisted. Romeo, the machomachine, came through unscathed. We unshipped the tool kit for an Allen key to correct Juliet's headset. No love lost. Extra tight this time.

Ahead lay the last long slope up the crater rim. We had no intention of even trying to cycle the first few yards. A short sit-down rest first. Then I grabbed my bike firmly by the crossbar and front down tube and hoisted it vertically in the air. Gently I lowered it down over my head to snuggle onto my shoulders: back wheel behind, front wheel dangling ahead of my navel, spiky chainrings playing footsie with my ear lobe, like the proverbial cast iron monad hung around my neck with black chastity belt locked on my throat.

We achieved that glorious feeling of bondage known well to all mountain bikes when, slogging up a steep slope, the high-tech bike with alloy fittings is reduced to a booby-prize plastic black toilet seat. All the anguish of yesterday's 3,000ft scree slog up the mountain from 15,500ft to the crater rim came flooding back. Memories of slipping and sliding in the torrential rains of the first afernoon in the wallows of the rain forest. 'Once more into the breach, my friend.' Nick looked repentent as we took the first of the final few steps towards the summit plateau.

That episode passed in a flash. In next to no time we were pedalling jubilantly across the final two hundred yards of nearly level snow to the summit cairn. All aches, pains and efforts were swept away. The view from our bicycles on the snow was over the clouds which stretched out all across Africa. We were the first people to truly test mountain bikes at high altitude on snow and ice. The highest cyclists in the world — that is to say; when we were up there we saw no others.

The Bicycles up Kilimanjaro expedition has raised £30,000 for the work of the charity Intermediate Technology, which develops tools and techniques which help the rural poor of the Third World to work themselves out of poverty using their own skills and resources. Specifically this money has been used to finance four water pumping windmills in the Sahel Belt.

Donations to: *BuK, Intermediate Technology, 9 King Street, London WC2E 8HW.*

Richard Crane

Chapter Eleven

Getting Started

SO far, this book has told the reader quite a bit about mountain biking — from how the sport originated, to where and what to do with your own off-road machine — even what clothes to wear when you're doing it.....That, you may say, is all very well, but some of us haven't even seen a mountain bike yet, much less owned one. There is, however, method in our madness — now that you've read all about mountain biking, you'll no doubt be itching to find out how to get into the sport and how to get hold of your own machine. The simplest advice is 'have a go'. If you like what you find, you can then think about splashing out on bicycle and equipment. This chapter couples an account of a first taste of the joys of mountain biking with a basic guide for the first-time buyer.

Elated, if saddle sore

By Stan Abbott

IT looked like any other house in the Pennine village — but the rows of mean-looking bicycles in a rack in the drive soon gave the game away as Barry and I arrived in Upper Cumberworth. The early summer morning carried the hint that the sun might just make amends for the worst that the rain had managed to throw at us the previous few days.

The bikes looked keen and eager for the off — Barry a little less so; and who could turn down the offer of a cuppa in the company of the Feast family cat and dog

Richard Feast — got on his bike

tribe?

Richard Feast is a man who took Norman Tebbit's advice and got on his bike to find work — after Mr Tebbit's Government took away his job. In fact the former civil engineer with the now defunct West Yorkshire County Council soon found himself the proud owner of no less than 15 bicycles after he pooled redundancy pay, council grant aid and an MSC Enterprise Allowance to turn pleasure to business.

As the owners of Ryedene Mountain Bikes, Richard, 37, and his 34-year-old wife Diane are at the front end of endeavours to spread the fruits of Britain's blossoming tourist industry a little wider.

His backers at Kirklees council's Employment Development Unit believe ventures like Ryedene can help translate the fame brought to moors and valleys around Huddersfield by TV's Last of the Summer Wine, into a lasting benefit for the area.

The council's £3,500 interest-free Tourism Development Loan to the Feasts is aimed at making sure there is something to bring visitors back to 'Summer Wine Country' after they've seen Nora Batty's house from a day-trip coach window.

Our aim was to find out whether the fleet of rugged bikes with their 15-speed gears really could provide an ideal way to explore an area.

'It's the one real growth area in cycling,' said Richard as we mounted a collection of cycles with names like Rockhopper and Muddy Fox, exhibiting a healthy contempt for whatever obstacles the area's network of green lanes, drove roads and forgotten trackways cared to throw up.

Besides Richard and ourselves were computer technician Brian Goodman from Staines, Middlesex, and his accountant wife Mel, on a return visit to Ryedene.

Keen touring cyclists with appropriate machines of their own, they say the mountain bike enables them to reach the parts their ordinary touring cycles simply can not reach.

'It makes it possible to get away from very busy roads,' said Brian.

Pictures in a puddle — wave-making for the camera

'It gives you a lot more flexibility — you can start off on the road but if you see an interesting bridleway you can head off

along it whereas on a touring bike you would be worrying about buckling your wheels.'

For Barry and I the biggest worry was how our ill-prepared muscles would stand up to the challenge of scaling these Pennine slopes. I could think of lots of things that were likely to buckle long before anything on the bike.

The first impression of the Specialized Rockhopper was very reassuring — compared with my old five-speed, which is occasionally pressed into service to take me five miles to the station, the handling seemed light and positive. Trying the 'crawler' gear nearly caught me unawares as the front wheel rode into the air with what seemed like the lightest of touches on the pedals.Five or ten minutes on the road and I'd got the saddle nicely jacked up to maximise the machine's ability to convert toast and muesli into forward, nay upward, motion.

The attributes of the machine became fully apparent as we left the road for a track which climbed to offer a trans-Pennine view as from the roof of the world. The nobbled tyres stuck like glue in the muddy puddles and the Rockhopper was inducing a glowing feeling of the invincibility of machinekind in the face of nature. Back on the road, its very low bottom gear had me cycling up

• Picture on previous page shows
Richard Feast, followed by the
writer, Mel and Brian, with the
Holme valley in the background

hills I'd never have believed possible,
while Barry seemed to be struggling on the
Muddy Fox Courier....then we discovered
he'd got confused about which of the three
chain rings gave the lowest ratio!

On the open road across the plateau the
Rockhopper showed it could show a clean
set of knobblies to any bike as we moved
up the cogs and gave it full muscle. I knew
my own bike would have run out of gears
at much lower speed, while the rolling
resistance of those chunky tyres seemed to
have little effect on the Rockhopper's
desire to keep on freewheeling along the
level.

Our route descended a deeply rutted,
rock-strewn track which tested the rider's
nerve as much as the ability of the big wide
tyres and sturdy frame to absorb the
jarring jolts. Standing on the pedals saved

the backside and improved control to
negotiate the obstacles.

A meander through lush woodland past
quiet reservoirs to a welcoming pub at
Holme village added credibility to
Richard's claim that once people become
aware of the beauties of this 'green lung'
between the conurbations of West and
South Yorkshire and Greater Manchester,
they will come back for more.

The rain obligingly confined its cautious
return to the hour or so within those thirst-
quenching walls before we headed along
the byways for Holmfirth where the BBC
had evidently fixed it for Richard by
ensuring there was a film crew at work
outside Ivy's cafe.

As we began the long slog back to Upper
Cumberworth my butt began to complain.
I'd expected to find aches where I didn't
even know I had muscles, but here was my
saddle locating nobbly little bones deep
within the flesh on my buttocks. I made a
mental note to choose my saddle very
carefully when eventually I made good my
resolve to buy one of these beasts.

**The Muddy Fox Courier — now established as one of the most popular
mountain bikes around**

Buying a cross-country cycle

By David Wrath-Sharman

SOME people seem to find buying a cross-country cycle a very traumatic experience — probably because they have high hopes but little knowledge, then suffer from a thousand conflicting reports, ideas and concepts. They may fall prey to hard-sell techniques.

The first thing to make your mind up about when buying a bicycle for use across country, is precisely the type of riding you intend doing.

Almost any bike can be ridden across country with varying degrees of success and comfort. If you want to ride casually along our flatter bridleways and tracks, you don't need a special bike — you probably would be well served by just an ordinary shopper bike or three-speed roadster. It is well worth remembering that before the last war, the great majority of minor roads and byways were not metalled, and the old style roadster was expected to handle rough roads and tracks as a matter of course — and, after all, it is the American equivalent of our roadsters that gave birth to the mountain bike. That many of them still exist and are quite rideable after 40 or 50 years says a lot for their suitability. In fact with hub gears and fully enclosed chains, some even with hub brakes, they are arguably more suitable for our climate and terrain than the present day American inspired mountain bike — if only they weren't so heavy.

If you're a long distance tourist who rides mainly on the road, but you would like the facility of being able to ride off-road on occasions, then you would be better suited with a heavy touring bike, which has been specially set up with low gears, bigger tyres and cantilever brakes. Such bikes in the past, were known as rough-stuff bikes, and were made with wider clearances around the tyres and more room for mudguards. They were popular in the Fifties, with many custom builders making them. There are at least two custom builders who will make such bikes today, and so would most others if given the correct instructions. There are one or two of the more upmarket production touring bikes that would do the job quite well if modified a little.

If you've decided that you really want a mountain bike or cross-country bike, you still have to make up your mind about your intended use as they vary far more than road bikes. These bikes can be categorised very roughly as: city bike, off-road bike or trials bike. All the categories overlap, there are no hard and fast rules and compromises abound. There will never be a perfect bike to fulfil all functions for all people, although some bikes might get pretty close to it for certain individuals. Having said all that, there are aspects of a bike's design which will make it more suitable for one application than another. As with all compromises, enhancing one attribute detracts from another, so you have to be very sure what you want your bike for. To help you sort out the innumerable variations of frame design and componentry we will briefly look at the broad requirement of each type.

The city bike is a very popular machine which appeals to many people who want a comfortable and safe bike mainly for road use. Tougher than any road machine that has been available in the past, it has fat, comfort giving, relatively puncture free tyres. The trend is towards narrower, smoother tyres than those fitted to purer off-road bikes. The handling should be fast and responsive, but capable of manoeuvering through traffic at slow speed and with narrow handlebars to suit. In this context the shorter the wheelbase and chainstay length the better, but it is not critical. Ground clearance is not a priority, so a low bottom bracket might be seen as an advantage as it reduces the straddle height of the crossbar. Really low gears are not so necessary, so the gear range can be biased towards the high side. Light in weight, the bike should be capable of fast acceleration, coupled with reliable progressive brakes. It is ideally suited to the stop-start of the city.

A bike built to these specifications is still very usable for general off-road riding, its ability only being limited by the low bottom bracket, the tyre type and the clearances in muddy conditions. Fitted with knobbly tyres the city bike would make an almost ideal off-road racing machine.

The off-road bike ranges from something akin to a city bike with knobblies, to the short, high trials bike. The final choice depends wholly on the sort of riding you want to do. For general off-roading, a long wheelbase and chainstays gives a softer ride with less pitching, but tends to be slower and more cumbersome. A shorter wheelbase offers greater speed and manoeuverability, but perhaps a harsher ride. Fat knobbly tyres are almost standard to cope with loose sand, mud and rocks. Far superior traction can had with short chainstays, but it is difficult to provide adequate mud clearance between the stay and tyre unless custom made. A recent development is the use of 24" rear wheels which enables the building of short stays without the clearance problems. The short

stays offer good traction but the small wheels offset some of this and require greater effort in soft conditions. They are slower overall. All experience to date shows that the bigger the wheel diameter,the smoother the ride, with better traction for less effort.

For serious long distance riding in all weathers, it is necessary to have enough clearance to fit mudguards, though the younger image-conscious element would probably not agree, as it is very unfashionable to use mudguards in America.

Such is fashion, but this is England with a quite different climate, and what is supposed to be attractive about a mud-spattered rider escapes me. Many American bikes are limited with regard to mudguard clearance for this reason. As ground clearance is all important, short cranks and higher bottom brackets are favoured. This leads to a taller bike with the problem of straddling the crossbar, so small frames and sloping crossbars with long seat posts are becoming more and more popular.

The gear system must be strong, fast and utterly dependable, with really low close-ratio gears. This is best achieved with the smallest chainrings on a triple set-up. The latest machines are using indexed gear systems wich really take the guess work out of gear changing, which is particularly useful for off-road riding.

Ideal handling needs to be predictable and viceless: a good off-road bike should be almost able to steer itself over rough ground. Head angles these days are steeper than the First Generation bikes, but with the industry standardising on 2" fork offset, some bikes with steepish head angles are a bit of a handful for the inexperienced on fast, bumpy downhills. Riding position on the latest machines is more upright with higher set, narrower

Saracen's Conquest, with hand-made Reynolds frame, sells at around £660

bars than the First Generation bikes used to be, which is a lot less demanding on the wrists and back.

Needless to say, a reliable braking system is paramount. The various forms of cantilever rim brakes are fine for most riding in the dry, but their performance leaves a lot to be desired in the wet. In muddy conditions, the braking may be almost non-existent, not to mention the damage done to the rims. The most realiable braking is offered by hub brakes, though some people are put off by the slightly greater weight,which is far less than imagined and is easily offset by reducing weight in other, less important areas. The most important advantages of hub brakes are consistent braking no matter what the conditions, and a soft progressive action without snatch, enabling you to stop on wet slippy surfaces without skidding or losing control. Buckled wheels become a problem of the past and no damage is caused to the rims or tyre sidewalls. Hub brakes need far less attention and the shoes need replacing infrequently compared with rim brake blocks. As they are still not popular they are not yet widely available, but a few manufacturers are beginning to offer bikes fitted with hub brakes as standard.

The trials bike is for the totally committed off-road rider. It is not widely popular and probably never will be. Trials bikes are really specialist machines — they are usually short wheelbased, have very high bottom brackets, limited gear range, high-set handlebars and very small frames with extremely low crossbars. The wheels range in size from 20" through 24" to 26" or even 28", and head angles from 74° to 68°. They are usually fitted with cantilever brakes, though one of the most versatile uses hub brakes. They are capable of extra-

ordinary feats in experienced hands. Pure trials machines are often very individual and are usually custom made, but a few manufacturers are offering machines that could fit into this category with a few modifications.

As can be seen from these classifications, a city bike comes very close to the all-round every day bike, for commuting, and for light off-road riding. With a higher bottom bracket and medium width bars it is potentially the best compromise for the new rider. However the shorter, higher, off-road bikes are often faster on and off-road and are less tiring to ride over long distances.

Having sorted out your needs the next thing to do is to work out the available budget, as this is going to influence your choice more than anything else. It must be borne in mind that the loads to be encountered when off-road riding are many times that found on the road. Any cost-cutting on strength and quality will soon be revealed if the bike is ridden hard, and the effects of frame or component breakage are potentially more severe off-road. If you want quality and reliability you must be prepared to pay for it. I'm often surprised by people saying they think bikes, particularly mountain bikes are expensive. Yet one of the more upmarket machines doesn't cost as much as the average hi-fi or colour television, or a pair of skis and boots for that matter. After all, your life and limbs depend on your bike. It will be expected to perform in the most atrocious conditions and could well be used day after day, year after year, and could carry you to the ends of the earth. So remember you only get what you pay for.

All the lower priced bicycles (below £250) are going to have pretty much the same specifications, the only real difference being the colour and graphics. This is a natural result of having to keep the prices down, where component choices become limited. With bicycles at these prices, it's very much more important where you buy it from — who assembled it — than who manufactured it.

Ask around locally for a reputable dealer who knows about mountain bikes. If you take advice from a shop you must remember that they have a vested interest in selling the models they stock and may not be entirely forthcoming about other models, or simply may not know enough about mountain biking in general to advise you correctly. Mountain bikes are not just fat tyred road bikes. Off-road machines are much more complicated, so it's as well to talk to as many mountain-bikers as possible to find out their opinions about their own bikes, but remember that the information will be personal and possibly biased, so sift out the nonsense and listen for what is relevant for you.

Also consider buying a secondhand bike to start off with. It is a good idea to hire a mountain bike for a day or two, or try different types to find what suits you. Some hire companies sell the same bikes as they hire. There is no better way to see how a particular model has fared over a period of time than riding a bike that has been on hire.

If you're interested in buying an expensive machine, I would suggest that you wait until you are more experienced at riding across country and can judge correctly for yourself which particular qualities of a bike will suit your riding style and needs. Paying a lot of money doesn't automatically mean that the bike will suit you better. In fact the more expensive the machine the greater the possible choices so its even more import-

ant to know what you are doing. If it's a custom bike that you have your heart set on, you had better have a lot of riding experience to be able to answer all the questions that any custom builder worth his salt will ask you in order to build your dream machine.

That'll do nicely thankyou — custom-built Highpath machine at a cool £1,500

103

Chapter Twelve

Mountain Bikes — Set to Dominate Cycling

by Tom Bogdanowicz

WHEN the first edition of this book appeared, mountain bikes were still an insider cult; off-road riders were considered slightly eccentric and their bicycles a bit unusual. Some pundits predicted that it was all a passing fad. They were wrong: mountain bikes have not gone away — they are fast becoming the most popular type of bicycle sold.

The past year has seen dozens of mountain bike features in the daily press; two new mountain bike magazines *Mountain Biking UK* and *Mountain Biker* have been launched; several mountain bike books have been published; and assorted new fanzines have appeared. Television has covered mountain bike competitions and big sponsors are taking an interest in the newly popular sport.

Most importantly, mountain bikes are selling in large numbers — not just to off-road enthusiasts but also to those new to cycling. As beginners have discovered, mountain bikes, with their straight handlebars, comfortable brakes and click-shift gears, are much more user-friendly than racing bikes — their stylish colours and lightweight equipment make them more sporty and attractive than roadsters.

Bike Design

The boom in mountain bikes has led to a proliferation of mountain bike varieties — street mountain bikes, racing mountain bikes, touring mountain bikes, junior mountain bikes. Many manufacturers supply bikes in every category. Some of the differences between the categories are cosmetic, some are a matter of money and some are very real practical distinctions.

To understand the differences between contemporary mountain bikes you have to look beneath the paint job at the geometry, the tubing and the components.

The original off-road geometry debate, described in the first chapter of this book, centred around frame angles and wheelbase. You'll be glad to hear that the debate has, at long last, been settled. Most MTBs, whether custom made or off the peg, have a 73-74° seat angle, a 70.5-71° head angle, sub-17" chainstays, and a 41-42" wheelbase.

Custom frames tend to vary the seat angle a little to suit the customer and some touring and downhill machines have a 70° head angle. But, basically, steep angles rule and the slack angled (69° parallel) long wheelbase (42"-plus) machine has become extinct.

The reason is that frames with steeper angles are more versatile — they are good for climbing and cornering as well as for rapid descents: riders are now more skilled at handling the livelier frames on downhills. Short chainstays are prefered because they put the rider's weight further over the rear wheel: this gives a better grip when climbing. Current variations in mountain bike geometry focus on top tube length, stem length and bottom bracket height. Altering any of these measurements by an inch makes a big difference. The basic variations are as follows:

Racing: 73-74/71 angles, 16.5-16.9 chain stays, top tube 3-3$^1/_2$" longer than seat tube, 125-140mm stem, 11$^1/_2$-12" bottom bracket.

Street riding: 73/71-72 angles, 16.9 stays, top tube 2-3" longer than seat tube, 90-125mm stem, 11$^1/_2$-11$^3/_4$" b.b. Touring: 73/70-71 angles, rest as street riding.

Note the big differences in top tube and stem length. Racers like to be stretched low over the front wheel for streamlining and balance — on some custom racing machines you will see road-type flat stems for an even lower, flatter position. Casual riders prefer a more upright position with a high stem and a shorter top tube (it's the street and touring machines that would benefit from sloping top tubes not the racing bikes).

Manufacturers don't make a big fuss of the racing/street riding differences because they want racing glamour to spill over onto their street bikes; some companies even build their street bikes with racing geometries. When buying an MTB don't be swayed by colour schemes, make sure the bike suits your riding style.

Although the geometry does affect performance, some of the other recent 'improvements' are primarily cosmetic. Wishbone seat stays, straight forks and twin down tubes have all been introduced in an effort to make bikes more distinctive. MTB buyers are very fashion-conscious and 'this year's model' has to look different.

The one really useful alteration in frame design for off-road cycling is the sloping top tube. As many a rider will testify, sloping top tubes prevent painful injuries when falling. Most custom bikes built in Britain have sloping top tubes and several major manufacturers now build production bikes with sloping top tubes. If you plan to do serious off-road riding this design is worth checking out.

Materials

Steel is still the material most frequently used in frame construction but aluminium and composites are increasingly popular, while titanium tops the weight-watching scales.

The American aluminium pioneers, Cunnigham and Klein, have been followed by a host of manufacturers led by Cannondale, Trek and Diamond Back. Most, but not all, of the new aluminium frames have over-size tubes to make them as stiff as steel frames. Aluminium brazing techniques have improved substantially cosmetically and recent quality frames have almost flawless fillets at tube joints.

When they were first introduced, composite frames had problems with the joints: you cannot weld or braze composite tubes. Glues, special lugs and assembly methods have improved but experts are still not convinced about the long term durability of jointed composite frames. One design which avoids this problem is the innovative Kestrel composite frame which is made from a single mould. If composite frames are to succeed then it is likely that they will take this form.

Titanium is light, rust free and stiff but diabolically expensive to buy and equally expensive to weld ($1,500 titanium frames are not uncommon). Most of the existing titanium MTB bikes come from a single source: Merlin Frames in the USA. Gary Fisher, of Fishercycles, has promised his own production titanium bike but supplies will take a while to reach Britain. Considering the price of titanium it is unlikely that it will ever become a popular framebuilding material.

In an effort to stem competition from the new materials, steel tube manufacturers have been forced to become more inventive. By using steels with high tensile strengths (1,100 N/mm² or more) tube makers have been able to supply tubes with thinner walls which are very light (approximately 5lbs for a 20" frame) but which are still quite stiff.

Two of the manufacturers have achieved this by heat-treating the tubes (Reynolds 753 and Tange Prestige); and one manufacturer, Columbus, is using a new steel alloy called Nivacrom. Columbus, an Italian tube producer, has also produced a tubeset with a larger diameter and with variable cross-sections to counteract torsional stresses at the bottom bracket and head tube (MAX).

These newly developed steel tubesets for mountain bikes are being used for most of the off-road racing frames. Racers like the predictability and durability of steel and they often ride custom-made frames. Most custom builders only produce steel frames.

Components

Now that the basic style of mountain bikes has settled down component manufacturers no longer need to revise the design of every component each year. The major concern is to produce cheaper versions of established components (both

Sun Tour and Shimano produce components in at least three different price ranges).

Nonetheless, aggressive competition has pushed the big players, Shimano and Sun Tour, to produce at least one or two major innovations every year. One company which chose to enter the fray in 1988 with a completely new range of components, was Campagnolo. The launch of Campagnolo's all-new Euclid group was the equivalent of a Royal blessing for mountain biking. The two horse race of previous years was over.

It was 1987 that was undoubtedly the year of indexed gear shifting. For those who have been away for a year of two and don't know what SIS or Accushift or Synchro means, I should explain that indexed gears enable you to shift gear by moving the gear lever a click stop in either direction: no adjustment, no missed shifts. At least that's the theory: on the road the theory is borne out; in thick mud, performance deteriorates, but recovers after a clean-up.

Indexed shifting was pioneered by Shimano on racing bikes but it has been on mountain bikes that indexing has really taken off. Sun Tour and Campagnolo have followed Shimano with indexed systems of their own. The great advantage of indexed gears has been the simplification of all those gear changes for beginners.

In 1988, and the latter part of 1987, there was a fashion-conscious preoccupation with the U-brake (a beefed-up version of the old braze-on centre pull brake) and the roller-cam brake. Following Californian style, most 1988 bikes sported a cantilever on the front fork and a U-brake or roller cam underneath the rear stays. The reason given for this arrangement was that the more powerful rear brakes had to be mounted on the less flexible chain stays rather than the seat stays. What the manufacturers failed to consider was that away from the sunny hills of California a rearbrake underneath the chain stays was more effective as a mud collector than as a brake.

Common sense prevailed in time and early 1989 saw the return of that old favourite: the cantilever — front and rear. But not just any old cantilever. Two manufacturers, Scott-Pedersen of the USA and Sun Tour of Japan, introduced the self-energising (SE) cantilever.

This is an ingenious system which uses the wheel's forward motion to exert a braking force through the brake pads. As the brake blocks grip the wheel they are

Scott's self-energising cantilever

pulled inwards on spiral bosses. The system produces extremely powerful but controlled braking. Its only existing rival in the power stakes is the hydraulic brake — models have been produced by Magura and Mathauser. But riders are concerned about the problems of repairing hydraulic brakes in harsh terrain, so we may have to wait for the lightweight hub brake to rival

the SE system (the small British company, Swallow, was about to put its hub brake design into production at the time of writing).

Shimano's major contribution to 1989 off-road bikes was the 'Hyperglide' free-wheel (manufacturers have discovered that to sell a new product that looks almost identical to an old product you have to give it a new name — hence hyperglide, SLR, SE, SIS, Synchro etc). Hyperglide sprockets, which have contoured guides to ease upward shifts, really do work — changes are so smooth that it almost takes the fun out of having 21 gears (both Shimano and SunTour have raised the number of rear sprockets to seven).

Shimano's '89 package also includes the re-introduction of a little known fad of the mid-80s: short two-finger brake levers. These are very convenient on bumpy downhills when you need two fingers to keep a sure grip on the bar and two to use the brake lever. Pairing Shimano levers with SE brakes may prove an effective combination.

When Campag entered the off-road market the racing fraternity had to acknowledge that mountain biking had arrived. Gossip about the Campag off-road group, Euclid, bubbled for a year before the product was unveiled at Cologne in 1988.

It took a further six months for the goodies to arrive in the shops. Like so many Italian goods, Euclid exuded style: gleaming platinum sheen as opposed to the functional black of Shimano and SunTour.

Euclid's sleek appearance disguises its rugged construction. Campag designed the group with durability and reliability in mind. Interesting innovations incorporated

Euclid group on a Roberts Phantom

British Custom Mountain Bikes

Compared to the thousands of Taiwanese and Chinese production bikes sold, the custom bikes built in Britain are but a drop in the ocean. But it's the custom bikes that set the trends for the future.

And 1988 was a vintage year for custom machines. Alec Moulton unveiled his ATB Moulton: a bright yellow space-framed bike with knobbly 20" wheels and fitted with off-road equipment, apart from the caliper front brake. David Wrath-Sharman, the legendary off-road guru, went back to his roots and built an 'everything but the kitchen sink' bike based on the Cleland design.

The cycle included all of David's idiosyncratic inventions: special hub-brakes, asymmetric chainstays with a dishless rear wheel, multi-position handlebars, integral chainguard and bottom bracket bash plate, and much more. Outrageously expensive, but well received.

Some of David's ideas are gradually percolating into mainstream bike-building. Dave Yates' bikes for the Two Wheels Good team all incorporate extra wide bottom brackets, asymmetric chain stays and dishless wheels (I wonder when the major manufacturers will realise that wide bottom brackets and dishless wheels are the best design for mountain bikes). Yates' bikes also include all top tube cable routeings 'to keep them clear of mud'.

Chas Roberts, bike-builder to the rich and famous and mountain bike pioneer, has continued to be first off the mark with new tubesets and group sets. His Phantom MAX built with Columbus MAX tubes

into the Euclid group include a monoplanar U-brake (the interlocking brake arms are parallel to each other) which ensures shudder-free braking; brakelevers and gear levers that permit an almost infinite number of adjustments; a bottom bracket with an external grease hole; and allen key spring tension adjustment on the rear gear mechanism. All the components show evidence of functional design which caters for the mechanic as well as the rider: standard tools, easy access to bearings, straight-forward adjustment.

Campag's latest mountain bike is a further development of Euclid. It offers several competition-style options like tub finger brake levers, smaller pedals, cantilever brakes and separate gear levers. Centaur is priced below Euclid.

and fitted with the Euclid group set has been drooled over in several shops. From the same Roberts stable came the first 753 ATB frame in 88 and the lightweight ANIA mountain tandem in 1989.

Swallow Cycles, have expanded their field from custom bikes to include cycling clothes (a la Rohan) and are working hard on special components, such as hub brakes and new frames.

Off-Road Racing

The 1988 mountain bike racing season was a memorable one in many ways. After being in the doldrums for a several years, racing blossomed in 88. Sponsors came forward by the dozen and venues proliferated.

All the major races were dominated by two newcomers to mountainbiking: Tim Gould and Dave Baker. Both riders are cyclo-cross professionals and their race hardened fitness and skills secured them top positions in almost every competition they entered. But for a puncture Tim Gould might have carried off the World Mountain Bike Championship crown at first attempt. As it was his sponsors, Peugeot, had to be satisfied with third place while Michael Kloser won the championship.

The dominance of cyclo-cross riders in mountain bike racing has been the cause of some friction beween the sports. Mountain bikers don't like being thoroughly beaten by professional, and sometimes amateur, cyclo-cross riders while the cyclo-cross race organisers are disappointed to lose competitors who are attracted by the prizes, glamour and easy success in mountain bike races.

The current debate over rules, regulations and organisation of mountain bike racing was likely to reach a head by the end of the 1989 season. Mountain bike

The distinctive Moulton MTB

races would either have to put their own house in order or come to an arrangement with an outside body.

Off-Road Touring and Trail Riding

As the number of mountain bikes sold has increased, so the number of riders venturing off-road has gone up. Rides across deserts, mountains, glaciers and continents are becoming more common. Gone are the early days when the five or so British mountain bike enthusiasts would turn up in Wendover for a Sunday ride. Nowadays, hundreds of fluorescent devotees take to the muddy hills around the country while more restrained riders pedal along canals and bridleways.

Unfortunately, large groups of off-road cyclists can create problems. Horse riders and walkers find it difficult to pass them and farmers object when they venture onto footpaths or private land. The issue has hit several newspapers and magazines and is a potential threat to the growth of mountain biking.

Among some riders, an addition to the off-road code has gained acceptance: keep the groups to single figures. If we don't act ourselves someone else will. I hope that the next edition of this book does not have to have warnings written across the front.

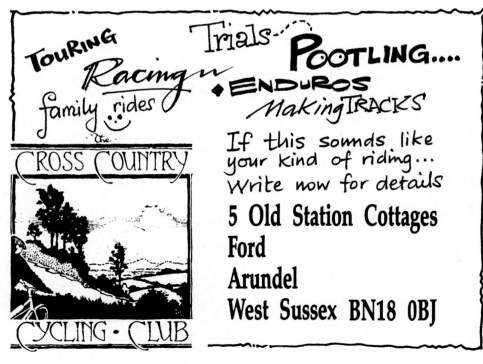

Chapter Thirteen
Directory

Compiled by David Wrath-Sharman
Where telephone numbers are not included, it is usually
because the business prefers postal contact.

Custom frame-builders

Peter Tansley
Alternative Engineering
8 Goldsmith Street
Heavytree
EXETER EX1 2RB

Charles Ralph
Alves Framesets
2 Earnside Cottages
ALVES
Moray TV36 0RB
Tel 034385 662

Tom Board
Board Framesets
20 Penton Street
LONDON N1

Dave Clark
Clark Frames
'Dorney'
Victoria Gardens
BIGGIN HILL
Kent TN16 3DS
Tel 01 778 7714

Simon Davey
Simon Davey Cycles
48 Saxon Road
St. Werburgh's
BRISTOL BS8 9UG
Tel 0272 541268

Dave Wrath-Sharman
Highpath Engineering
Felin Hafodwen
Cribyn
LAMPETER
Dyfed SA48 7ND
Tel 0570 470 075

Jim Harrison
J & C Engineering
Station Yard

APPLEBY
Westmoreland CA16 6UL
Tel 07683 51870

Bob Jackson Cycles
148 Harehills Lane
LEEDS LS8 5BD
Tel 0532 493022

Harry Quinn
Harry Quinn
Lightweights
Ivy Tower Farm
St Florence
TENBY SA70 8LP
Tel 0834 871531

Tony Oliver
Oliver Framesets
Maes Merdydd Uchaf
AMLWCH
Anglesey

Chas Roberts
Roberts Racing Frames
89 Gloucester Road
CROYDON
Surrey CR0 2DN
Tel 01 684 3370

Dave Russell
Dave Russell Cycles
16-18 Chavey Road East
SLOUGH
Berks SL1 2LU
Tel 0753 29880

Peter Bird
Swallow Cycles
2 Stannetts
Laindon North Trading
Centre
LAINDON
Essex SS15 6DJ
Tel 0268 418655

Custom ATB builders

Cleland
Cleland Cycles
5 Old Station Cottages
Ford
ARUNDEL
West Sussex BN18 0BJ
Tel 0243 553404

Davey
Simon Davey Cycles
48 Saxon Road
Saint Werburgh's
BRISTOL BS8 9UG
Tel 0272 541268

Highpath
Highpath Engineering
Felin Hafodwen
Cribyn
LAMPETER
Dyfed SA48 7ND
Tel 0570 470075

Horizon
Two Wheels Good
35 Call Lane
LEEDS LS1 7BT
Tel 0532 456867

Overbury
Overbury's Cycles
138 Ashley Road
BRISTOL BS6 5PA
Tel 0272 557924

Paris
Avis Cycling & Leisure
21 Clerkenwell Road
LONDON EC1M 5RD
Tel 01 250 1534

Quinn
Harry Quinn Lightweights
Ivy Tower Farm
St Florence
TENBY SA70 8LP
Tel 0834 871531

Roberts
Roberts Racing Frames
89 Gloucester Road
CROYDON
Surrey CR0 2DN
Tel 01 684 3370

Swallow
Swallow Cycles
2 Stannetts
Laindon North Trading
Centre
LAINDON
Essex SS15 6DJ
Tel 0268 418655

Yates
Dave Yates
2 Station Road
South Gosforth
NEWCASTLE upon TYNE
NE3 1QD

Special transmission systems

Chris Bell
Cycle Transmissions
162 Bloomfield Road
Brislington
BRISTOL BS4 3QX
Tel 0272 770626

Special luggage systems

Freedom Bikepacking
Packers Cottage
Albion Street
EXETER EX4 1AZ
Tel 0392 219560

Production ATB manufacturers, importers and wholesalers

Ammaco
Ammaco BMX Ltd
Unit 1F
Deacon Trading Estate
Aylesford
MAIDSTONE
Kent ME20 7SP

B.H. Boland
Bolton Stirland Ltd
Boland House
Nottingham South Ind. Est.
Ruddington Lane
Wilford
NOTTINGHAM
NG11 7EP

British Eagle
British Eagle Ltd
PO Box 6
Eagle Cycle Works
Mochdr
NEWTOWN
Powys SY16 4LD

**Cannondale/Eclipse/
Fisher**
Chainsport
40/42 Clapham High Street
LONDON SW4 7UR

Cinelli
T W Rutter (Acc) Ltd
Unit L Rudford Ind Est.
Ford Road Ford
LITTLEHAMPTON
West Sussex BN18 0BD

Dawes
Dawes Cycles Ltd
Wharf Road
Tyseley
BIRMINGHAM
B11 2EA

Evans
F.W. Evans
77/79 The Cut
Waterloo
LONDON SE1

**Falcon/Holdsworth/
Marlboro/Claud Butler**
Falcon Cycles Ltd
PO Box 3
Bridge Street
BRIGG
South Humberside
DN20 8PB

Giant
Giant UK Ltd
Plessey Business Park
Technology Drive, Beeston
NOTTINGHAM
NG9 2ND

Horizon
Two Wheels Good
35 Call Lane
LEEDS LS1 7BT

Bob Jackson/Merlin
Bob Jackson Cycles Ltd
148 Harehills Lane
LEEDS LS8 5BD

Marin
ATB Sales
Whitworth Road
St LEONARDS-ON-SEA
East Sussex TN37 7PZ

**M.B.K/Diamondback/
Emmelle/Puch**
Moore and Large & Co Ltd
Crown House
664-668 Dunstable Road
LUTON
Bedfordshire LU4 8SD

Mercian
Mercian Cycles
7 Shardlow Road
ALVERSTON
Derbyshire DE2 0JG

Moulton
Alex Moulton Ltd.
BRADFORD-ON-AVON
Wiltshire BA15 1AH

Muddy Fox
Muddy Fox Cycles Ltd
331 Athlon Road
WEMBLEY
Middlesex HA0 1BY

Orbit
Orbit Cycles
Unit 8
Peartree Ind. Park
Peartree Lane
DUDLEY
West Midlands DY2 0GY

Overbury
Overbury's Cycles
138 Ashley Road
BRISTOL BS6 5PA

Peugeot
Cycles Peugeot (UK) Ltd
Edison
Edison Road
BEDFORD
Bedfordshire MK41 0HU

Raleigh
T I Raleigh Ltd
Triumph Road
NOTTINGHAM
NG7 2DD

Reflex
Reflex Mountain Bike Co
The Gate Studios
Station Road
Elstree
BOREHAMWOOD
Hertfordshire WD6 1DE

Renegade
Renegade Cycles
22 Duke Street Hill
LONDON SE1

Ridgeback
Madison Cycles
4 Horseshoe Close
LONDON
NW2 7JJ

Roberts
Roberts Racing Frames
89 Gloucester Road
CROYDON
Surrey CR0 2DN

Saracen Kettler
Saracen Cycles Ltd
PO Box 86
LEAMINGTON SPA
Warwicks CV32 6SB

Scott
Bert Harkins
Racing Scott USA
Unit 6
The Townsend Centre
Houghton Regis
DUNSTABLE
Bedfordshire

Specialized
Caratti Sport Ltd
49 Waverley Road
Yate
BRISTOL BS17 5QZ

Swallow
Swallow Cycles
2 Stannetts
Laindon North Trading
Centre
LAINDON
Essex SS15 6DJ

Tushingham
Tushingham Cycles Ltd
Glasshouses Mill
PATELEY BRIDGE
North Yorkshire
HG3 5QH

Dave Yates M Steel
M Steel Cycles
2 Station Road
South Gosforth
NEWCASTLE
upon TYNE
NE3 1QD

Specialist ATB shops

SCOTLAND

City Cycles
30 Rodney Street
EDINBURGH EH1 1QH
Tel 031 557 2801

Cycle Logic
366 Great Western Road
Kelvinbridge
GLASGOW G4
Tel 041 339 4933

Edinburgh Bicycle Co-op
5/6 Alvanley Terrace
Whitehouse Loan
EDINBURGH EH9
Tel 031 228 1368

Robin Williamson
26 Hamilton Place
EDINBURGH EH3 5AU
Tel 031 225 3286

WALES

Rob Lally
Broad Street
HAY-on-WYE
Powys
Tel 0497 820891

Steves Cycles
33-35 High Street
BANGOR
Gwynedd
Tel 024 8361 400

Schmoos Cycles
Lower Oxford St.
SWANSEA
W Glamorgan
SA1 3JG
Tel 0792 470698

NORTH

Bicycle Doctor
68 Dickenson Road
Rusholme
MANCHESTER M14
Tel 061 224 1303

Claude Crimes
Fountain Roundabout
CHESTER
Cheshire
Tel 0244 381177

Davies Brothers Cycles
6-8 Cuppin Street
CHESTER
Cheshire CH1 2BN
Tel 0244 319 204

Peter Darke Cycles
244 Fulwell Road
SUNDERLAND SR6 9EU
Tel 0783 485575

Harry Hall Cycles
25-33 Hanging Ditch
MANCHESTER M4 3ES
Tel 01 832 1369

Dave Heron Cycles
6 Neville Street
DURHAM CITY
Tel 091 384 0287

Grange Cycles
Under Butterfingers
Main Street
GRANGE-OVER-SANDS
Cumbria
Tel 04484 2745

Ghyllside Cycles
The Slack
AMBLESIDE
Cumbria
Tel 05394 33592

Settle Cycles
The Cycle Shop
Duke Street
SETTLE
North Yorks BD24 9DJ
Tel 072 92 2216

M Steel Cycles
2 Station Road
South Gosforth
NEWCASTLE upon TYNE
NE3 1QD
Tel 091 2851251

Summit Cycles
167 Bolton Road
BLACKBURN
Lancashire BB2 3QJ
Tel 0254 54230

Two Wheels Good
35 Call Lane
LEEDS LS1 7BT
Tel 0532 456867
and
140-142 West Street
SHEFFIELD
Tel 0742 720207

York Cycleworks
Lawrence Street
YORK YO1 3BN
Tel 0904 26664

Upton Cycles
139 Ford Road
Upton WIRRAL
Merseyside L49 0TH
Tel 051 678 2277

SOUTH WEST

Avon Valley Cyclery
Under the Arches
36-37 Dorchester Street
BATH Avon BA1 1SX
Tel 0225 461880

Barrettos Bikes
7 Dean Hill
The Broadway, Plymstock
PLYMOUTH PL9 9TP
Tel 0752 408338

Overbury's Cycles
138 Ashley Road
BRISTOL BS6 5PA
Tel 0272 557924

**Plymouth MTB
Company**
Queen Annes Battery
PLYMOUTH
Tel 0752 268328

Poole MTB Centre
111 Commercial Road
Lower Parkstone
POOLE
Dorset
Tel 0202 741744

MIDLANDS

Castle Cycles
15-17 Boar Lane
Newark
NOTTINGHAM
NG24 1AJ
Tel 0636 79893/4

**Edison Lightweight
Cycles**
83 Highstreet
Clowne
CHESTERFIELD
Derbyshire
Tel 0246 812878

Longmynd Cycles
40a Sandford Avenue
CHURCH STRETTON
Shropshire
Tel 0694 722367

Walton Street Cycles
78 Walton Street
OXFORD
Tel 0863 511531

SOUTH EAST

**Aylesbury Two
Wheel Centre**
120 High Street
AYLESBURY
Bucks HP20 1RB
Tel 0296 415215

**Channels Mountain
Bike Centre**
Back Lane
Little Waltham
CHELMSFORD
Essex
Tel 0245 441000

Cycle System
45b Bridge Street
PINNER
Middlesex HA5 3HR
Tel 01 868 2918

B & L Stevens
51 Walton Street
Walton-on-the-Hill
TADWORTH
Surrey KT20 7RR
Tel 073781 3127

Ben Hayward Cycles
69 Trumpington St
CAMBRIDGE CB2 1RJ
Tel 0223 352294

Broadway Cycles
65 The Broadway
STONELEIGH
Surrey
Tel 01 393 3256

Cycleland
27 Widmore Road
BROMLEY
Kent BR1 1RW
Tel 01 460 4852
and
18 Windmill Street
GRAVESEND
Kent
Tel 0474 533748
and
90 High Street
CHATHAM
Kent
Tel 0634 417539
and
5 Gabriels Hill
MAIDSTONE
Kent
Tel 0622 52537
and
Epping Forest ATB Centre
24 Lindsey St.
EPPING
Essex
Tel 0378 77660

Finch and Son
43 Bell Street
REIGATE
Surrey
Tel 07372 42163

Get on your Bike
5 Bridge Street
GODALMING
Surrey
GU7 1HY
Tel 0486 20055

Kingston Cycles/Evans
48 Richmond Road
KINGSTON-UPON-
THAMES
Surrey KT5 5EE
Tel 01 549 2559

Portswood Cycles
3 Old Saint Deny's Road
Portswood
SOUTHAMPTON
Tel 0703 556470

Terry Wright Cycles
41-43 Bridge St
Deeping
St. James
PETERBOROUGH
Cambridgeshire
Tel 0778 344051

LONDON

Avis Cycling & Leisure
21 Clerkenwell Road
LONDON EC1M 5RD
Tel 01 250 1534

Brixton Cycles
433 Coldharbour Lane
LONDON SW9
Tel 01 733 6055

Cycle Logical
136/138 New Cavendish
Street
LONDON W1
Tel 01 631 5060

Covent Garden Cycles
2 Nottingham Court
LONDON WC2H 9AY
Tel 01 836 1752

Bike UK
Lower Robert Street
Charing Cross
LONDON WC2
Tel 01 839 2111
and
244 Pentonville Road
Kings Cross
LONDON N1
Tel 01 833 3917
and
40/42 Clapham High Street
Clapham
LONDON SW4 7UR
Tel 01 622 1334
and
273/279 High Street
Acton
LONDON W3 98T
Tel 01992 2877

CHAS ROBERTS

THE BUILDER THE PROFESSIONALS TRUST

OUR LEGENDARY OFF-ROAD RACER
THE WHITE SPIDER

"The White Spider features a multitude of details that distinguish a state-of-the-art bike from even the best production machine" BICYCLE ACTION 1988

Why is there a waiting list of off-road riders who are prepared to pay for a White Spider mountain bike?
Every WS is custom made: That means we will alter not just the seat and top tube lengths but the frame angles, the bottom bracket height, the chainstay length, the fork rake etc.
Every WS is immaculately fillet brazed by hand: Only a few builders in the world, most of them in the US and UK, can make lugless frames that are both beautiful and strong.
A sloping top tube is standard: This is the optimum design for serious off-road riding (and falling off).
WS are built out of the best tubes that we can buy: The latest Columbus Nivacrom OR tubes provide a perfect balance of strength and weight. We can also use 753ATB or Tange Prestige.
Every WS has an oversized head tube: For strength and solid but sleek rear brake bridge--it dosen't budge.
Specially reinforced tubes can be fitted for riders who want to mount powerful brakes on the seat stays.
You get to chose any colour: we find that this is the major problem, so think hard before you visit.

Every WS, and every Roberts, is built at our workshop in Croydon using skills which have built champions bikes for two generations.
When you are ready for the best give us a call 01 684 3370 (Fri-Sat please).
Send a large SAE for the definitive mountain bike catalogue,
it includes cheaper models!!
Roberts Cycles 89 Gloucester Road, Croydon, Surrey CR0 2DN

Specialist ATB shops (cont)

BIKE UK (Cont.)
YHA shop
14 Southampton Street
Covent Garden
LONDON
WC2E 7UR
Tel 01 497 2299

F.W. Evans
77/79 The Cut
Waterloo
LONDON SE1
Tel 01 928 4785

London MTB Centre
557-561 Battersea Pk Road
LONDON SW11 3BL
Tel 01 223 2590

Mosquito Bikes
10 Bradbury Street
Dalston
LONDON N16
Tel 01 249 7915

On Your Bike
22 Duke Street Hill
London Bridge
LONDON SE1
Tel 01 378 6669

Regent Cycles
136 Kentish Town Road
LONDON
NW1
Tel 01 485 1310

South Bank Bicycles
194 Wandsworth Road
LONDON
SW8 2JU
Tel 01 622 3069

Swift Cycles
15 Dartmouth Road
Forest Hill
LONDON
SE23 3HN
Tel 01 699 2961

ATB hire and holidays

SCOTLAND

Castle Moil Centre
Kyelakin
Isle of Skye
Tel 0599 4164

Central Cycle Hire
13 Lochrin Place
EDINBURGH
Tel 228 6333

**Glentress Mountain
Bike Centre**
Venlaw High Road
PEEBLES EH45 8RL
Tel 0721 20336

Hill Craft
73 Main Street
Tomintoul
ABERDEEN
Tel 09752 207

Perthshire MTBs
31 Taymouth Drive
KENMORE
Tayside PH15 2HS

Robin Williamson
26 Hamilton Place
Stickbridge
EDINBURGH
EH3 5AU
Tel 031 225 3286

Strathlene Hotel
KIRKMICHAEL
Perthshire
Tel 0250 81347

Continued over

117

ATB hire and holidays (cont)

WALES

Clive Powell Mountain Bikes
The Mount
RHAYADER
Powys LD6 5DN
Tel 0597 810585

Pedalaway
Trereece Barn
Llangarron
ROSS-ON-WYE
HR9 6NH
Tel 098984 357

Red Kite Mountain Bikes
Gordon Green
Neuadd Arms Hotel
LLANWRTYD WELLS
Powys LD5 4RG
Tel 06913 236

NORTH

Chester MTB Centre
St Marks Road
Saltney
CHESTER
Tel 0244 671212

Cyclecraft
12 Morningside
LANCASTER LA1 1FR
Tel 0524 62742

Cycleventure
The Old Mill, Brigsteer
KENDAL
Cumbria LA8 8AT
Tel 04488 558

Keld Bike Centre
Keld Lodge
Keld
RICHMOND, N Yorks
Tel 0748 86259

Lakeland Mountain Bikes
Low Green
STAVELEY
Cumbria LA8 8LA
Tel 0539 821748

Lakeland Leisure
Spring Gardens
Station Precinct
WINDERMERE
Cumbria LA23 1AN
Tel 09662 4786

Lowick MTB Hire Centre
Old Spade Forge
Lowick Green
ULVERSTON
Cumbria LA12 8DY

MTB Dales Tours
39 Rowan Court
CATTERICK VILLAGE
North Yorkshire DL10 7RS
Tel 0748 811885

The North Country Shop
Rise Hill Mill
Dent
SEDBERGH
Cumbria
Tel 05875 370

Rydene Mountain Bike Hire
Unit 8b
Lower Sunny Bank Mills
Sunny Bank Road
MELTHAM
West Yorkshire HD7 3LL
Tel 0484 850074

MIDLANDS

English (Bike Breaks)
Freepost
Albert Street
TELFORD
Shropshire TF2 9AS
Tel 0952 610158

Longmynd Cycles
40 A Sandford Avenue
CHURCH STRETTON
Shropshire
Tel 0694 722367

Cadence Cycle Hire
Foregate Street
Railway Station
WORCESTER
Tel 0905 613501

SOUTH WEST

Adventure Cycles
of Devon
Ian Shields
Newinton Lodge
Dudley
NEWTON ABBOT
Devon TQ13 0JX
Tel 0626 852154

Avon Valley Cyclery
Under the Arches
36-37 Dorchester Street
BATH Avon
BA1 1SX
Tel 0225 61880

Bicycle Beano
59 Birch Tree Hill
Clehonger
HEREFORD
Tel 0981 251087

Cadence Cycle Hire
Foregate Street
Railway Station
WORCESTER
Tel 0905 613501

Keith Willis
Off Road Rentals
17a Gorlestone Road
Branksome
POOLE
Dorset

Outdoor Adventure
Atlantic Court
WIDEMOUTH BAY
Cornwall EX23 0DF
Tel 028885 312

Saddle Tramps
11 Athelston Road
Tuckton
BOURNEMOUTH
Dorset
Tel 0202 431920

Wessex Cycling Holidays
23 Elwell Street, Upwey
WEYMOUTH
Dorset DT3 5QF
Tel 0929 463170

SOUTH EAST

Action Packs
Robin Cottage
Stones Lane, Westcott
DORKING
Surrey RH4 3QH
Tel 0306 886944

Channels Mountain Bike Centre
Back Lane
Little Waltham
CHELMSFORD, Essex
Tel 0245 441000

Muddy Tours
742 Great West Road
ISLEWORTH
Middlesex
Tel 01 568 0407

> **The information contained in this directory was, to the best of our knowledge, correct at the time of publication.**
> **The publishers, however, can accept no liability for any inaccuracies or omissions.**

Bike handling classes

Geoff Apps
5 Old Station Cottages
Ford
ARUNDEL
West Sussex BN18 0BJ
S.A.E. please

Clive Powell
Clive Powell Mountain
Bikes
Blaencwm Farm
Llanwrthwl
LLANDRINDOD WELLS
Powys LD1 6NU
S.A.E. please

Bike Breaks
Freepost
Albert Street
TELFORD
Shropshire
TF2 9AS
Tel 0952 610158

Tom Sillis
1 Santon House
Santon Downham
IPSWICH
Suffolk
IP7 0TT
Tel 0842 812359

Magazines

Bicycle Action
331 Athlon Road
WEMBLEY
Middlesex HA0 1BY

Bicycle Magazine
and **Mountain Biker**
PO Box 381
Mill Harbour
LONDON E14 9TW

Making Tracks
5 Old Station Cottages
Ford
ARUNDEL
West Sussex BN18 0BJ

Mountain Biking UK
Woodstock House
Luton Road
FAVERSHAM
Kent
ME13 8HQ

Outdoor Action
38-42 Hampton Road
TEDDINGTON
Middlesex
TW11 0JE

Rough Stuff Journal
(See Rough Stuff
Fellowship)

National cycling clubs

BCCA
The British Cyclo Cross
Association
208 Eccleshall Road
SHEFFIELD S11 8JD

CCCC
Cross Country Cycling
Club
5 Old Statuion Cottages
Ford
ARUNDEL
W. Sussex BN18 0BJ
S.A.E Please

CTC
Cyclists' Touring Club
Cotterell House
69 Meadrow
GODALMING
Surrey

> NOTE — The various
> national bodies can
> supply lists of local
> member clubs

MBC
Mountain Bike Club
J Torr
3 The Shrubbery
Albert Street
TELFORD

RSF
Rough Stuff Fellowship
61 Southbank Road
SOUTHPORT
Lancashire PR8 3NE
S.A.E. Please

Useful addresses

Byways and Brideways
Trust
9 Queen Anne's Gate
LONDON SW1

Council for
National Parks
45 Shelton Street
LONDON
WC2H 9HJ

Friends of the Earth
377 City Road
LONDON
EC1V 1NA

Council for the Protection
of Rural England
4 Hobart Place
LONDON
SW1W 0HY

Countryside Commission
John Dower House
Crescent Place
CHELTENHAM
Gloucester, GL50 3RA

Open Spaces Society
25a Bell Street
HENLEY-on-THAMES
Oxfordshire
RG9 2BA

Survival Aids
Morland
PENRITH
Cumbria CA10 3AZ

Youth Hostels Association
8 St Stephens Hill
ST ALBANS
Herts AL1 2Y

Index to Directory Section